ROUTLEDGE LIBRARY EDITIONS:
MODERN FICTION

Volume 4

STORIES OF RESILIENCE IN CHILDHOOD

STORIES OF RESILIENCE IN CHILDHOOD

The Narratives of Maya Angelou, Maxine Hong Kingston, Richard Rodriguez, John Edgar Wideman, and Tobias Wolff

DANIEL D. CHALLENER

LONDON AND NEW YORK

First published in 1997 by Garland Publishing Inc.

This edition first published in 2020
by Routledge
2 Park Square, Milton Park, Abingdon, Oxon OX14 4RN

and by Routledge
52 Vanderbilt Avenue, New York, NY 10017

Routledge is an imprint of the Taylor & Francis Group, an informa business

British Library Cataloguing in Publication Data
A catalogue record for this book is available from the British Library

ISBN: 978-0-367-26004-0 (Set)
ISBN: 978-0-429-34150-2 (Set) (ebk)
ISBN: 978-0-367-33404-8 (Volume 4) (hbk)
ISBN: 978-0-367-33420-8 (Volume 4) (pbk)
ISBN: 978-0-429-31974-7 (Volume 4) (ebk)

Publisher's Note
The publisher has gone to great lengths to ensure the quality of this reprint but points out that some imperfections in the original copies may be apparent.

Disclaimer
The publisher has made every effort to trace copyright holders and would welcome correspondence from those they have been unable to trace.

STORIES OF RESILIENCE IN CHILDHOOD

The Narratives of Maya Angelou, Maxine Hong Kingston, Richard Rodriguez, John Edgar Wideman, and Tobias Wolff

DANIEL D. CHALLENER

GARLAND PUBLISHING, Inc.
New York & London / 1997

Library of Congress Cataloging-in-Publication Data

Challener, Daniel D.
Stories of resilience in childhood : the narratives of Maya Angelou, Maxine Hong Kingston, Richard Rodriguez, John Edgar Wideman, and Tobias Wolff / Daniel D. Challener.
p. cm. — (Children of poverty)
Includes bibliographical references and index.
ISBN 0-8153-2800-1 (alk. paper)
1. Authors—American—20th century—Biography—History and criticism. 2. Poor children—United States—Biography—History and criticism. 3. Resilience (Personality trait) in children. 4. Narration (Rhetoric) 5. Autobiography. I. Title. II. Series.
PS129.C42 1997
810.9'0054—dc21
[B] 97-11822

Printed on acid-free, 250-year-life paper
Manufactured in the United States of America

To Melinda

Who gave me the support, encouragement, and love
that I needed to write this

and

to Brandon, Skye, and Dakota
who gave me wonderful reasons to finish.

Contents

Acknowledgments

This study would never have been started or finished without the unwavering support of George Monteiro. He allowed me to work at my own pace and write what I had to write. I owe him far more than an acknowledgment.

Ted Sizer consistently offered encouragement and thoughtful advice on drafts of this book. A man whose work is transforming the American educational system, he was never too busy to offer me his ideas or send an encouraging note.

Matt Aldrich, first a fine student and then a great friend, read every page with extraordinary care, offered insights and ideas, and helped to untangle more than a few sentences.

Lorraine Mazza offered encouragement and a compassionate ear from my first day at Brown to my last. She is a good advisor and friend.

Also in Brown University's English Department, I wish to thank Thadious Davis, who offered useful criticism of my chapter on Maya Angelou, William Keach, who expressed interest in my topic and supported my decision to leave the department while writing, and Elizabeth Kirk, who made it possible for me to teach a special course that explored many of the books and ideas in this study.

At Providence Blueprint for Education, I am grateful to Edward D. Eddy for six years of wise counsel, good friendship, and his extraordinary example of donating thousands of hours solely for the benefit of Providence's children.

At Garland Press, I owe many thanks to Tania Bissell, who patiently encouraged me as I missed one deadline after another, and Chuck Bartelt, who worked a technological miracle with my computer discs.

Much of my thinking and many of my ideas come from students who have been in my classes. They are too numerous to mention by name, but surely I owe a debt of gratitude to them and those schools: Brown University, George Washington High School in New York City, Hope

Central, and Mt. Pleasant High Schools in Providence, The Peddie School in Hightstown, New Jersey, Johnson and Wales University, and Trenton Public Schools. These students taught me that all children can be resilient if the adults know enough and care enough.

Finally, I owe my greatest thanks to my parents, who gave me endless support and love and every opportunity and educational advantage imaginable, and to my wife, who throughout the too many years it took to write this book encouraged me and kept telling me that finishing was a worthy goal. Without them, I would have given up long ago.

Stories of Resilience in Childhood

I
Resilience, Autobiography, and Children

What helps a child overcome extraordinary obstacles? Why do some children surmount many difficulties and go on to live fulfilling lives while other children who face similar difficulties end up living desperate, sad lives? What helps children beat the odds? What builds resilience in children?

These are critically important questions, yet for too long social scientists, doctors, psychologists, and teachers have studied children who failed and tried to figure out what caused the failure. They identified high school dropouts, for example, and then worked backwards to try to find out what caused the student to leave school. Only relatively recently has much effort been made to understand what creates success—what helps children overcome obstacles and beat the odds.

This book is an effort to understand better what contributes to a child's "success" and "resilience." Our source of information will be autobiographies of childhoods—autobiographical stories written by adults remembering their difficult childhoods. This is not a research study with scientifically randomly selected participants who were matched with a control group. Nor is this a series of case studies created from the answers to a rigorous and consistent protocol of questions asked by trained researchers who interviewed a representative sample of resilient children. Rather, this is an attempt to read and listen to five stories about resilient children and see what they tell us about supporting children and building resilience.

I will argue, of course, that these stories offer a depth and breadth uncommon to the articles on child development and building resilience in publications like *Journal of Adolescent Research* or the *Journal of Personality and Social Psychiatry*. I believe that as we look at the story that John Wideman tells or that Tobias Wolff tells we can get a new and different vista on "resilience" and childhood. This is not to say that Wideman's story tells us more than an article in the *Journal of Adolescent Research.* It is, however, simply to say that *Brothers and Keepers* can tell us something about childhood and resilience worth thinking about. And, I believe that at the close of this century, with more than one in every five children growing up in poverty and with more than half of these children living with only one parent, we must try to understand and support the forces that help children overcome the many obstacles that they now so commonly face.

I. THE AUTOBIOGRAPHIES OF RESILIENT CHILDREN

Toni Morrison's novel *The Bluest Eye* presents the antithetical realities of childhood in America: for some children it is heaven and for others it is hell. Morrison prefaces each chapter of her novel with excerpts from the classic American reader *Fun with Dick and Jane.* These passages describe the mythical childhood that American children who grew up in the 1950's were all supposed to have. A family consists of a mother and a father, a son and a daughter. They live in a small white suburban house that has a nice front lawn and is surrounded by a white picket fence. They are all happy:

> Here is the family. Mother, Father, Dick, and Jane live in the green-and-white house. They are very happy . . . See Mother. Mother is very nice. Mother, will you play with Jane? Mother laughs. Laugh, Mother, laugh. See Father. He is big and strong. Father, will you play with Jane? Father is smiling. Smile, Father, smile. (7)

Morrison juxtaposes this vision of childhood with her own story about the horrific childhood of Pecola Breedlove, the central character of *The Bluest Eye*. Pecola's childhood is nothing short of a nightmare. With her parents and her brother, Pecola lives in a tiny one room apartment that is filled with wornout furniture. Her parents fight all the time, often venting their anger by beating Pecola and telling her that she is ugly. At school she is humiliated by her classmates, who wear nicer clothes and get more praise from the teacher. Ultimately,

Pecola is raped by her father and the resulting baby dies at birth. Shunned by all in the community, Pecola retreats into silence and, finally, madness. We last see her, alone, picking through garbage at a dump on the edge of town.

Depending on one's sensibilities, *The Bluest Eye* is either powerful or hopelessly melodramatic. One is either moved by the pathos of Pecola's dreadful childhood or scornful of the extremes of Morrison's plot and prose. Yet, regardless of how one reacts to Morrison's first novel, there are remarkable similarities between some of the scenes in Morrison's novel and Maya Angelou's childhood autobiography, *I Know Why the Caged Bird Sings*. Indeed, if we look at both works side by side, it seems as if Morrison could have based some scenes from her novel on some scenes from Angelou's childhood.

No doubt, Pecola Breedlove and Maya Angelou have much in common. Poor, Black, and female, both girls suffer through many of the same indignities. Both girls are abandoned by their parents, humiliated by white children and white adults, and made to feel as if they are inferior to white children. In the face of such desperate situations, both girls dream of being different, of looking like the white children who are praised in their towns. Pecola dreams of having blue eyes and blond hair. She believes that if she looks like the American dream child she will be treated accordingly and her problems will disappear:

> It had occurred to Pecola some time ago that if her eyes, those eyes that held the pictures, and knew the sights—if those eyes of hers were different, that is to say, beautiful, she herself would be different . . . If she looked different, beautiful, maybe Cholly would be different, and Mrs. Breedlove too. Maybe they'd say, "Why, look at pretty-eyed Pecola. We mustn't do bad things in front of those pretty eyes. . . .
>
> Each night, without fail, she prayed for blue eyes. Fervently, for a year, she had prayed. Although somewhat discouraged, she was not without hope. To have something as wonderful as that happen would take a long, long time. (40)

In much the same way, Maya Angelou dreams the same dream of looking like the idealized blond haired, blue eyed white child her community seems to love. In fact, Angelou begins *I Know Why the Caged Bird Sings* by recounting one of her many versions of this dream:

> As I'd watched Momma put ruffles on the hem and cute little tucks around the waist [of a new dress], I knew that once I put it on I'd look like a movie star . . . I was going to look like one of the sweet little white girls who were everybody's dream of what was right with the world . . .
>
> Wouldn't they be surprised when one day I woke out of my black ugly dream, and my real hair, which was long and blond, would take the place of the kinky mass that Momma wouldn't let me straighten? My light-blue eyes were going to hypnotize them, after all the things they said about "my daddy must of been a Chinaman" . . . because my eyes were so small and squinty. Then they would understand why I had never picked up a Southern accent, or spoke the common slang, and why I had to be forced to eat pigs' tails and snouts. Because I was really white and because a cruel fairy stepmother, who was understandably jealous of my beauty, had turned me into a too-big Negro girl, with nappy black hair, broad feet and a space between her teeth that would hold a number-two pencil. (1-2)

While the girls share similar dreams, they also share the same nightmare. Both girls are raped. Pecola is raped by her father; Maya Angelou is raped by her mother's frustrated lover. In the aftermath, both girls come to believe that they somehow deserved to be raped. Full of shame and self-hatred, both girls retreat into silence and depression.

Despite similarities of race, gender, and experience, Pecola Breedlove and Maya Angelou ultimately end up in very different places. Whereas Pecola Breedlove's childhood ends in tragedy, Maya Angelou's childhood ends in triumph and hope. Whereas *The Bluest Eye* culminates with Pecola's total isolation from her family and society, *I Know Why the Caged Bird Sings* ends with Maya's successful reunion with her family and clear demonstrations of her autonomy and competence.

Why the antithetical endings? What is it that enables some children like Maya Angelou to overcome the odds while other children like Pecola Breedlove do not? More specifically, what can autobiographies about childhood tell us about the resilience of children who face multiple challenges? What can we learn about the characteristics and forces that allow children like Maya Angelou to emerge victorious from difficult childhoods? Are there similar supports that help resilient children like Maya Angelou and Richard Rodriguez, Tobias Wolff and Maxine Kingston? Is there one type of support that all resilient children must have? Is there one obstacle that is insurmountable? In sum, what is it that help builds resilience?

In the pages that follow, I examine five autobiographies of children who grew up in the United States. Like *I Know Why the Caged Bird Sings*, each of these autobiographies is about a child who faced considerable hardship yet ultimately prospered and became an autonomous and competent adult. In my title and throughout the pages that follow, I refer to these children as "resilient" children. *The American Heritage Dictionary* defines "resilient" as "the ability to recover quickly from illness, change, or misfortune; buoyancy." This is something of what I have in mind, but so too is the definition Emmy Werner uses in *Vulnerable but Invincible*, her path-breaking longitudinal study of disadvantaged children from the Hawaiian island of Kauai. In this study, Werner defines resilience as "the capacity to cope effectively with the internal stresses of their vulnerabilities . . . and external stresses" (4). Werner goes on to develop a precise process for determining which of her subjects are "resilient" children; they have faced at least four of ten predictive factors that Werner defines carefully and by age eighteen each has demonstrated certain specific positive traits, as measured by interviews and psychological tests.

In deciding which autobiographies qualified as the autobiography of a resilient child, I used a much less rigidly quantifiable process than did Dr. Werner. I defined resilience in broader, simpler, more personal terms; for me a resilient child was one who faced considerable challenges—more than those of an average child—yet ultimately was able, as an adult, to function as an independent, caring individual. Using this broad definition, I found a plethora of autobiographies of resilient children to choose from.

To narrow down my choices, I made several decisions. First, I decided that I wanted to examine diverse childhoods and thereby give myself the opportunity to think about many different issues and many different experiences. Consequently, I chose five autobiographies that recounted childhoods that were fundamentally different from each other. Not coincidentally, four of these five works are written by non-white writers. In part, this reflects my aim to examine diverse childhoods, for being African-American, Mexican-American, or Chinese-American usually insures, for better and for worse, that your childhood will be different from that of many other children. This over-representation of minority children also reflects the harsh reality that in the United States, Black, Asian, and Hispanic children too frequently have the "opportunity" to be resilient because their minority status forces them to face a daunting list of obstacles that large numbers of white children never face.

William Andrews has argued, convincingly, that the minority writer's sense of being marginalized is a powerful impetus to write autobiography and thus be heard. This, Andrews contends, helps to explain the wealth of autobiographies written by African-American authors (195-210). Certainly, this may explain why I found such a disproportionate number of autobiographies of resilient minority children to choose from. However, I hope that the over-representation of stories about children of color does not mislead any reader about the demographics of children who face extraordinary challenges. In fact, in the United States, a majority of children facing the most commonly cited characteristics of disadvantage are white. According to the Children's Defense Fund, almost two thirds of all poor children in America are white. White children make up more than half of the population of children who live in one parent homes, drop out of school, give birth to children while in their teens, and get arrested for violent crimes.

Another criterion I used in choosing autobiographies was publication date: I wanted to examine as contemporary a collection as possible. Consequently, each of the autobiographies in this study was published after 1970. With the single exception of *I Know Why the Caged Bird Sings*, each tells the story of a child who grew up in the latter half of the 20th century. For the most part, this decision reflects not only my area of literary interest, but also my professional training and experience. Over the last decade I have had the opportunity to teach and work with children labeled as "disadvantaged" in New York City, Trenton, New Jersey, and Providence, Rhode Island. In the late 1980's, through the generosity of The Ford Foundation and the U.S. Department of Education, I conducted three years of research on "at-risk" children (and, thus, I know first hand how much research was done working backwards, from children who "failed"). And most recently, through the generosity of several Rhode Island foundations and corporations, I have had the opportunity to study Providence's public schools and their impact on children. Working with these five autobiographies provided me a fruitful opportunity to draw from and expand on my understanding of the lives of contemporary American children.

Having mentioned recent publication and diversity of experience as criteria for my choices of autobiographies, I must acknowledge that the most important criteria for selecting these five autobiographies was personal taste. Quite simply, these five autobiographies are, in my opinion, the most interesting and most powerful of the more than fifty autobiographies of twentieth century American children that I considered. Why I favored these autobiographies often depended on the experiences described—some autobiographies just seem more interesting to me, just as some lives are more interesting than others. But in selecting autobiographies, the voices that told the autobiographies were often very important in my selection process. A compelling and fascinating voice tells each of these autobiographies, one that not only intrigued me but also helped me to think in other ways about the childhood of the storyteller.

Having acknowledged how important "voice" was in my selection process, I should warn my reader that in each succeeding chapter I look at the voice that tells the story and then briefly discuss that voice and how it tells its tale. I do so advisedly. The general status of stylistics—as a critical method—has been challenged by recent theoretical critiques. Long gone are the days when critics could blithely assert that form compels meaning and that the frequent use of non-finite progressives reveals the one true meaning of an autobiography. Yet, my goal in attempting brief discussions of voice is to provide another way of talking about these works, another way of describing what I hear in these autobiographies. George Dillon is right, I think, when he argues

> One engages in formal analysis to specify and articulate one's own response and perhaps to share it with others . . . Under this model, we can hope the results will be interesting, striking, or suggestive, enhancing our sense of how the parts can be orchestrated and

> bringing to notice things we had not seen before. If that's the game, then it is not a question of it being too easy or hard to play, and the proper response to a successful piece of stylistic analysis would be "I see" and not "You've proved your point." (75)

Certainly, what I highlight in my brief discussion of voice reveals my own interpretation of the work and my own biases and background as Talbot Taylor, in *Linguistic Theory and Structural Stylistics*, argues it must (107). As more than one of my readers has pointed out, my interpretations reveal a lot about me and how I understand childhood and children.

Although I will discuss the qualities of the voices of these autobiographies, ultimately I will spend more time discussing a fascinating commonality in all of them: each autobiography recounts, at considerable length, how each child struggled to escape being silenced. These autobiographies document how these children, in one way or another, struggled to "speak," to use words in order to establish an identity that was acceptable to themselves and break away from an identity that others had tried to impose on them.

To be sure, these struggles differ dramatically. In *The Woman Warrior*, Maxine Hong Kingston recounts her struggle to speak her mind and thereby reject the silence, complacency, and degradation that her family and community impose on girls. In *I Know Why the Caged Bird Sings*, Maya Angelou recounts her struggle to speak at all, to break the silence that being raped imposed on her. In *Hunger of Memory*, Richard Rodriguez recounts his struggle throughout his childhood to find a voice that was acceptable to Anglo-Americans yet did not alienate himself from his Mexican-American family. In *Brothers and Keepers*, John Edgar Wideman recounts his struggle to craft a voice that was acceptable in the world of the Ivy League and did not reveal his upbringing in Pittsburgh's low-income community of Homewood. And in *This Boy's Life*, Tobias Wolff recounts his struggle to express his needs and reject the notion that boys should suffer in silence.

The importance of speaking out should not be surprising. Finding a voice (and, in a larger sense, establishing an identity) is much of what growing up is all about. The passage from childhood to adulthood almost always requires children to establish their own identity and, in so doing, articulate their similarities and their differences from their parents and their community. Yet, for the children whose autobiographies make up this study—Maya Angelou, Maxine Hong Kingston, Richard Rodriguez, John Edgar Wideman, and Tobias Wolff—commanding language and finding a voice pose challenges far more difficult than what most children face. For these children, there are any number of obstacles facing them: poverty, the difference between the language spoken at home and the language spoken by the dominant culture, the absence of a parent, racism, the gross failure of teachers and schools, the monolithic nature of the community they live in, or the many differences between the culture of their family and the dominant culture of the United States. All of these obstacles silence many children and deny them an authentic, authoritative voice.

Of course, each autobiography is testimony—hard evidence—that all five children eventually won their struggle, not only survived childhood but also found a voice that allowed them to "speak" and find a place in U.S. society. In this sense, each of these autobiographies is a "success" story, for unlike Pecola Breedlove, each writer has escaped from silence and is able to tell her or his story. Yet while each writer escapes Pecola Breedlove's sad fate, several authors document the tremendous loss that they accepted by speaking with a "new" voice. In *Hunger of Memory*, for example, Richard Rodriguez's ability to speak and write "Ivy League English" earns him tenure track jobs at elite universities but also leaves him unhappy and isolated from his Spanish speaking family. In *Brothers and Keepers*, John Edgar Wideman discusses at length the cost of his decision to speak with the voice of an Ivy League educated Rhodes Scholar and ignore the voice of his street-wise brother.

Having written all this, let me close this section by re-stating my highest goal for this study. Since the end of the 1980's, much of the mass media has come to realize the costs of a decade of greed and now has become obsessed with the frightening predicament of America's children. Newspaper articles, sensationalized television programs, radio talk shows have all shouted out that our next generation of children is in profound peril. Yet the media has taken very little time to go beyond recognizing the eye-catching symptoms of the problem and discuss, with thought and true concern, the remedies. The highest goal of this dissertation is to pay attention to what it is that enables children to succeed and be resilient despite many challenges.

II. THE AUTHORITY OF AUTOBIOGRAPHY

In a 1986 appearance at Brown University, John Wideman, after reading exclusively from his just published collection of short stories, *Fever*, was questioned exclusively about *Brothers and Keepers*, which had been published two years earlier. Exasperated, he wondered aloud, "Why is it that Americans are so fascinated with the facts of autobiography and ignore the truths of fiction?"

The answer to Wideman's question is not a simple matter. Many critics have argued that Americans have had a long love affair with autobiography because autobiography reinforces some of the values that many Americans hold most dearly: independence and individualism. The Declaration of Independence, the U.S. Constitution, and the Bill of Rights, probably the three most revered documents of American history, all spell out quite carefully the rights of individuals. From my window, I can see atop the Rhode Island State House the symbol of the state of Rhode Island: the independent man. He signifies the state's deeply held belief in the rights of an individual to be wholly independent of the demands of government and church. Indeed, Ronald Reagan dominated a decade of U.S. history by using persistent allusions to the value of rugged individualism. Autobiography, in many minds, speaks to these values and the importance of the individual.

Another part of the answer to Wideman's question relates to the deep desire of many Americans to "get ahead." Since Colonial days, financial and personal success (measured by money, power, and status) have been goals of many Americans. Beginning with *The Autobiography of Ben Franklin* and continuing through Lee Iococo's autobiography, many Americans have been fascinated with the "facts of autobiography" because they believe these facts will help them succeed in the competitive culture of the United States.

For the most part, however, the privileged status of autobiography stems from a widely held perception that autobiography, more so than any other genre, reveals the truths about life. If one function of literature is to reveal "verities of life," what genre is better suited than autobiography? Unlike fiction, autobiography does not spring from the imagination of the author but rather from the facts of life. The authority of the autobiographer is the linchpin to such arguments. Who better than an autobiographer to reveal the facts of her or his life?

Recently, however, the authority of the autobiographer has been severely challenged. Many literary and linguistic theorists have suggested that autobiography does not have nearly the authority that many have believed for so long. Citing studies on memory and pointing out the limitations of language, these theorists have dramatically changed how many view autobiography and, indeed, how I read the autobiographies of children discussed in the chapters to follow.

Part of the privileging of autobiography has always been based on the belief that autobiographers have information that they (and they alone) are able to remember and reveal to readers. Much recent research, however, has called into question the ability of humans to do what autobiography demanded—namely remember the details of a life. Too much happens in any life for an individual to remember very much very accurately. Moreover, this research documents that when individuals can't remember what happened to them, they create (from their imagination) what is missing and then come to believe that what they made up actually happened. In summary, research reveals that human memory is far from reliable, and that what we "remember" is likely to be, at least in part, fabrication if not fiction.

The limitations of memory described above are important when one considers the task of writing a coherent life story. If, as the research shows, we regularly fill in missing details in accordance with suggestions made to us, it seems unlikely that an autobiographer can provide what autobiography promises—a seamless web of personal history that recounts verbatim conversations that occurred decades ago.

These deficiencies in human memory are even further problematic when one considers the writing of a full-length history of one's childhood. One needs only to try to remember a year of one's youth to recognize immediately the limitations of our ability to recall substantial portions of our young lives. Indeed, one needs only to try to recall independently any conversation in our youth to recognize the virtual impossibility of such a travail. When my students and I have tried to write about our respective childhoods, we have found ourselves very quickly engaged in filling in details and calling up friends, parents, siblings, and grandparents to get help. Whether we use our imagination or our contacts, we compromise our authority. Indeed, as many critics have argued, autobiography often times reveals a great deal about the *present* state of mind of the autobiographer.

Despite the problems presented by research on memory, essays on the ambiguity of language make even greater challenges to the authority of autobiography. Over the last twenty years, innumerable literary critics have tried to show the tendency of language not to reveal "truth" but rather to refer to itself and other, multiple, external languages and texts. They argue that most words have multiple meanings; if you put words with multiple meanings side by side, "meanings" grow almost exponentially. This line of argument has ultimately led "deconstructive" critics to declare that all texts have unlimited interpretations and thus an indeterminate meaning.

Vis a vis autobiography, Paul de Man, in "Autobiography as De-Facement," argues that because of the circularity of language, autobiography cannot and does not refer to the life of the subject but rather it ultimately refers to itself. According to de Man, autobiography tells the story of language and writing, not the story of a life:

> But are we so certain that autobiography depends on reference, as a photograph depends on its subject or a (realistic) picture on its model? We assume that life *produces* its consequences, but can we not suggest, with equal justice, that the autobiographical project may itself produce and determine the life and that whatever the writer *does* is in fact governed by the technical demands of self-portraiture and thus determined, in all aspects, by the resources of his medium? And since the mimesis here assumed to be operative is one mode of figuration among others, does the referent determine the figure, or is it the other way around: is the illusion of reference not a correlation of the structure of the figure, that is to say no longer clearly and simply a referent at all but something more akin to a fiction which then, however, in its own turn, acquires a degree of referential productivity? (920-921)

In essence, de Man proposes that autobiography really only reveals itself—not the life of the autobiographer—and thus is essentially "more akin to a fiction." Obviously, such an argument profoundly challenges the authority of autobiography and the concomitant belief that autobiography tells a true story.

The problems posed by research on memory and the arguments of deconstructive critics have led many scholars to contend that autobiography, at least as a source of authority about the life of its subject, is dead. In response to these scholars, others scholars have come to autobiography's defense. They have attacked de Man's assertion that autobiography is "more akin to a fiction" and tried to wrestle back a middling position for the authority of autobiography.

Philippe Lejeune has argued cogently and passionately that autobiography *can* tell truth and that an autobiographer's language *can* escape from itself and tell the story of the autobiographer's life. In "The Autobiographical Pact," Lejeune recognizes the intellectually appealing argument of the deconstructionists, yet asserts that there is an authority to autobiography that is undeniable:

> It's better to get on with the confessions: yes, I have been fooled. I believe that we can promise to tell the truth; I believe in the transparency of language, and in the existence of a complete subject who expresses himself through it; . . . I believe in the Holy Ghost of the first person. And who doesn't believe in it? But of course it also happens that I believe in the contrary, at least claim to believe it. Whence the fascination that Roland Barthes par Roland Barthes has held for me . . . "In the field of the subject, there is no referent." We *indeed know* all this; we are not so dumb, but once this precaution has been taken, we go on as if we did not know it. Telling the truth about the self, constituting the self as complete subject—it is fantasy. In spite of the fact that autobiography is impossible, this in no way prevents it from existing. (131)

Lejeune contends that the authority of autobiography springs from the unspoken pact between reader and autobiographer, a pact in which the autobiographer commits to telling the truth. Lejeune contends that this pact, a social contract of sorts, transcends the limitations of language that de Man and deconstructionists use to try to destroy the literal authority of autobiography.

James Olney has defended the authority of autobiography in a less spiritual but only slightly less moralistic manner. Olney argues that while language (and hence autobiography) cannot provide a one-to-one correlation to experience, language *can* provide a general sense of the self. Olney believes that autobiography functions much like metaphor and myth; it offers a hazy—but at its core accurate—view of what is. As John Paul Eakin points out, "For Olney, the exercise of autobiographical discourse is to be valued in the spirit that Socrates adopts toward his myth of the earthly paradise in the *Phaedro*: ' . . . either this or something very like it is a true account of our souls and their future habitation . . . this I think is both a reasonable contention and a belief worth risking; for the risk is a noble one" (*Fictions* 189-190).

Olney's allusion to metaphor and myth is, in my mind, particularly useful, for it arrives at some indistinct but actual middle ground between the argument for one-to-one correlation between autobiography and the autobiographer's life and the argument that there is essentially no relationship between life and autobiography. Indeed, as we discuss the autobiographies that make up this study, we will see that in fact there does seem to be a general sense of each author's life; the fluid interaction between each author's voice and the experiences forms, albeit in a hazy imprecise way, a general sense of childhood.

Moreover, Olney's view is particularly useful in this study of five childhood autobiographies because, as we look at these five autobiographies, we will recognize recurring similarities in many areas, particularly in areas that relate to the autobiographer's accounts about the importance of family, community, school, ethnicity, and language. Indeed, through a glass dimly we see experiences that are ostensibly different but are also ultimately quite similar. In short, the similarities between the story that Maya Angelou tells and Maxine Hong Kingston tells, the similarities between the story that John Wideman tells and Tobias Wolff tells are significant and provide, like myth and metaphor, a reinforcing sense of what these childhoods were like.

I must acknowledge a personal interest and angle here. I find as I examine the autobiographies of Maya Angelou, Maxine Hong Kingston, Richard Rodriguez, John Edgar Wideman, and Tobias Wolff I am struck by how much their stories support what so much research has shown to be generally true about the lives of the "resilient" children who live in the United States. Much excellent research has shown that families are tremendously important to the fate of children, that adults who truly care about a child change lives, that schools can paralyze or empower, that gender expectations can liberate or imprison, that churches and school basketball teams really can change a child's life, that racism still cripples children, that language can make or break young people. As I have read the childhood autobiographies of Maya Angelou, Maxine Hong Kingston, Richard Rodriguez, John Edgar Wideman, and Tobias Wolff, I have been struck again and again by how much their stories echo this research. To my mind the research and the stories thereby earn additional authority because they reinforce each other.

As one might infer from the preceding paragraph, I plan to take a truly inter-disciplinary perspective as I discuss each work, an approach that mixes literary criticism and adolescent development, autobiographical studies and sociology, stylistics and the literature of educational reform. Such an approach may lead some to complain that I have overlooked the limits of autobiography's authority. My goal, however, is to strike a middle ground, to pitch my theoretical tent close to James Olney's position that autobiographies offer a hazy metaphoric sense of what a child's life was like, if not what a case study would report. Like Philippe Lejeune, I do not deny the circularity of language or the limitations of memory. I do not contend that there is a one-to-one correlation between the text and the life. I am not so dumb. Nevertheless, I do believe that there is probably much greater danger in not giving autobiography any authority. Moreover, I believe that if we continue to spend most of our time proving that language is circular and that meaning is indeterminate, we will continue to spend too little time figuring out what we can do to improve the lives of children.

Over the last twenty years, deconstructive critics amply demonstrated their ability to deconstruct texts, to show the indeterminacy and thus the impotency of the very texts that their New Critical professors had asked them to worship. Like 1960's college students, deconstructive critics have stormed and overrun the loci of power of English Departments. Unfortunately, the very tenets of their own theory—that words have no determinate meaning—have too often rendered them unable to contribute anything of value to political or social agenda. Theirs is an agenda and a language so elite they have become isolated from all social causes. They have settled for publishing tenure-insuring book after tenure-insuring book, and for doing very little that affects the lives of children.

In *Protocols of Reading*, Robert Scholes (moving back away from his own earlier, warmer embrace of deconstruction) observes

> In particular, for the generation whose sensibilities were shaped by the 1960's, the anarchistic irreverence of deconstruction holds a profound attraction. For those who still remember the slogans of the past well enough to think of themselves as having sold out, as having been co-opted by the establishment, the verbal or textual posture offered by deconstructive discourse is almost irresistible. Its appeal is so strong because it allows a displacement of political activism into a textual world where anarchy can *become* the establishment without threatening the actual seats of political and economic power . . .
>
> The therapeutic effect of all this is far too obvious for anyone to condemn it outright. It does people good to feel radical and go around deconstructing things. And it is possible, as many writers have shown, to adapt the methodology of deconstructive analysis to secular or political ends. (65-66)

Scholes is right up until those final sentences, but then he is terribly wrong. To support deconstruction for its therapeutic effects, because it makes people feel good to feel radical, and to ignore the political implications of the theory is solipsistic and irresponsible at best. Scholes suggests many writers have shown that it is *possible* to adapt deconstructive analysis for political ends—and this may be so. Critics may have shown how deconstructive analysis could be used for political ends. But to suggest that critics or scholars or even the handful of policymakers and decisionmakers outside of the ivory tower who understand deconstruction have actually used deconstructive analysis to achieve any change, have any impact, in the status of the lives of America's children is sheer nonsense. Deconstructive critics have spent their time on other things. I defy anyone to prove otherwise.

My position is simple: I doubt that there may be something to be gained by "demolishing beyond hope of repair the machine of Western metaphysics," to quote the arch-deconstructionist himself, J. Hillis Miller (Campbell 25). And I believe quite fervently that there is a much more urgent need and much more to be gained by thinking about what these stories tell us about the needs of children. I therefore prefer to attempt to *construct* a discussion of what was and what is rather than attempt to deconstruct these autobiographies in order to show what wasn't and what isn't.

Ultimately, then, this study will focus on the lives of children. In so doing, I will try not to lose track of the important questions that deconstruction raises about the authority of autobiography, but I am committed to spending more energy trying to understand the lives of these children and what it is that made their childhoods difficult and what it is that made them resilient. To me, that is what matters. With some luck, this study will shed light on autobiography, fiction, childhood, resilience, children, and maybe even ourselves, desperate or resilient as we may be.

II
When A Whole Village Raises A Child: *I Know Why the Caged Bird Sings*

Over the last two decades, researchers from a host of different fields have begun to study why some children succeed despite extraordinary hardships and disadvantages. These researchers have taken a very different tack from many of their earlier colleagues who, as noted in the introductory chapter, primarily studied children who failed and tried to figure out what caused the failure. This new generation of researchers sees its field as not a study of pathology and failure but rather a study of resilience and success.

Over the last ten years, several of the leaders in this new field have begun to agree on an outline of key similarities amongst "resilient" children. In a widely quoted article entitled "Children in Poverty: Resilience Despite Risk," Norman Garmezy (one of the foremost of the resilience researchers) reviews the findings of many of his colleagues and asserts that researchers are consistently finding three broad similarities in the lives of resilient children. Garmezy defines the three similarities this way:

> 1. *temperament:* a resilient child has a high level of energy and is very active, is a good thinker with above average cognitive skills, and responds positively and warmly to adults within and outside of his or her family
>
> 2. *family:* a resilient child usually lives in a family marked by "warmth, cohesion, and the presence of some caring adult such as a grandparent who takes responsibility in the absence of responsive parents or in the presence of strong marital discord."

> 3. *external support:* a resilient child usually benefits from strong support from people and institutions outside of the child's family; these frequently include people involved with churches, teachers, parents of peers, coaches and adult leaders of youth activities.

Garmezy's summary is supported by the work of more than two dozen researchers, including Emmy Werner, whose work was discussed in the preceding chapter. Werner devoted her professional career to following, over a period of more than 40 years, a population of approximately 200 children born and raised on the Hawaiian island of Kauai. Reflecting on what four decades of study revealed about the characteristics of resilient children, Werner wrote in 1989 that

> Three types of protective factors emerge from our analyses of the developmental course of high-risk children from infancy to adulthood: 1) dispositional attributes of the individual, such as activity level and sociability, at least average intelligence, competence in communication skills (language and reading) and an internal locus of control 2) affectional ties within the family that provide emotional support in times of stress, whether from a parent, a sibling, spouse, or mate; and 3) external support systems whether in school, at work, or church, that reward the individual's competencies and determination and provide a belief system by which to live. (p. 80)

Obviously, Werner confirms Garmezy's trilogy of key attributes of resilient children: 1) personality and intelligence, 2) family strength, and 3) neighborhood and community support.

The final chapter of this study looks more closely at the commonalities of resilient children and what they tell us about how to help children. Before we get there, however, the chapters that follow offer five in-depth views of what builds resilience. Most immediately, the pages that follow examine the childhood of Maya Angelou. Beset by virtually every imaginable disadvantage—poverty, divorced parents, sexual abuse, racial discrimination—Angelou somehow survives and thrives. *I Know Why The Caged Bird Sings* provides not only an inspiring story, but also a useful framework for exploring the obstacles children face and how a united community can help a child overcome a daunting array of obstacles and develop the profile of resilience described by Norman Garmezy and Emmy Werner.

I. THE SILENCING OF MAYA ANGELOU

When they are but three and four, Maya Angelou and her brother, Bailey, are sent to live with their grandmother, who runs a general store in Stamps, Arkansas. Maya's mother and father are going through a calamitous separation and are unwilling to keep their children in the middle of their problematic lives. Unfortunately, Maya and Bailey's parents never explain to their children why they are being sent away, and, as children of divorced or separated parents usually do, Maya and Bailey assume that they have been sent away as a punishment for something terribly wrong that they have done. Maya believes that she has been rejected by her parents because of some severe personal failing; these emotions profoundly affect her childhood and are instrumental in beginning the series of events that will silence her.

As soon as she arrives in Stamps, Maya experiences a deep feeling of alienation and displacement. The townfolks initially regard her "without curiosity but with caution." When she is seen to be harmless, they close around her, "as a real mother embraces a stranger's child. Warmly, but not too familiarly" (4). This sense of being accepted but not deeply loved is apparent in the autobiography's opening scene. Here, Maya cannot remember the second half of the poem she is supposed to recite before the congregation of Stamps' Colored Methodist Episcopal Church. All she can remember are her opening lines

> What you looking at me for?
> I didn't come to stay.

These lines are emblematic of her sense of alienation (what are *you* looking at *me* for) and of the impermanence of her present home (I didn't come to stay.) Ironically yet appropriately, what she cannot remember are the poem's final two lines, which herald the Resurrection of Christ and the promise of love, eternal life and forgiveness. Humiliated by her forgetfulness, Maya runs out of the church—not back to her grandmother or other parishioners—and hides by herself. Her action and emotions bespeak her feeling that the parishioners are not her family but rather are part of a community that tolerates but does not love her.

Angelou ends her description of this scene by declaring

> If growing up is painful for the Southern Black girl, being aware of her displacement is the rust on the razor that threatens the throat. It is an unnecessary insult. (3)

The operative word here is displacement, for it is that sense of being shuffled around that permeates most of the early sections of Angelou's autobiography. Maya has little opportunity to feel settled or safe; her mother has sent her away, and she has no idea how long she will stay in Stamps. ("What are you looking at me for, I didn't come to stay.")

In "Building a Positive Self-Concept in the Black Child," Dr. Alvin Poussaint argues that the single most important element in developing a child's self-esteem is consistent caring from immediate family members. Poussaint writes that "the growing child requires love, protective care, and support from all members of her or his immediate family. With consistent caring, a child will develop strong feelings of belonging and worth. Infant care determines a child's primary core and most important identity" (27). Yet the opening pages of *I Know Why the Caged Bird Sings* document that Maya's mother and father are completely unable to provide "consistent caring" and love that a child needs. Indeed, after Maya's parents send her away, they have no contact with her for five years. They never visit her. They never write her. They never send her any indication that they are alive.

Maya rationalizes her parents' silence by holding to the belief that her parents are dead; she can make herself cry any time by picturing how her mother must have looked lying in her coffin. Then, when Maya is seven, she and her brother receive Christmas gifts from their mother and father. Their rationalization that they were sent away because there parents are dead is clearly wrong. They are devastated:

> The gifts opened the door to questions that neither of us wanted to ask. Why did they send us away? and What did we do so wrong? So Wrong? Why, at three and four, did we have tags put on our arms to

> be sent by train alone from Long Beach, California, to Stamps. Arkansas, with only the porter to look after us? (Besides, he got off in Arizona.) (43)

They are now absolutely convinced that they did something wrong and that is why they were sent away—but what did they do?

To make matters worse, Maya's mother sends a gift that increases Maya's sense of inadequacy, of not being what her mother wanted. Maya's mother sends "a doll with blue eyes and rosy cheeks and yellow hair painted on her head" (43). The doll embodies exactly what many of the white people in Stamps believe that Maya should be: a blue-eyed, blond haired little white girl. Living in Stamps, Maya has learned that such little white girls are the apple of society's eyes. Indeed, in the opening chapter of *I Know Why the Caged Bird Sings*, Maya reveals that she, in fact, dreams of looking like the doll her mother sends, of looking "like one of the sweet little white girls who were everybody's dream of what was right with the world" (1). Maya tells herself that one day she will wake from her "black ugly dream" and have long blond hair, light-blue eyes, and everyone will apologize to her for not realizing that she was really white and that a "cruel fairy stepmother, who was understandably jealous of [her] beauty had turned [her] into a too-big Negro girl" (2). The use of the words "black *ugly* dream" and "*cruel* fairy stepmother" underlines Maya's sense of the inherent undesireableness of being African-American. The primacy of its place in her autobiography—on the second page—indicates that the sense of being diminished by being African-American was a central element of Maya's young identity. The pain that the gift causes is apparent: Maya and Bailey tear the stuffing out of the doll the day after Christmas.

Stamps' racism contributes to Maya's sense of impotence and self-hatred. Again and again, Maya's African-American neighbors are threatened and forced to accept demeaning treatment because of their skin color. Maya attends a school that is vastly inferior to the school that white children attend. Her school is equipped with furniture and books that are passed down from the white children's school long after the usefulness of these items is gone. Maya and her classmates are steered out of "academic courses" and into home economics and farming classes in a not so subtle effort to prepare them to be the next generation of domestics and share croppers that the white citizens of

Arkansas will need to maintain their comfortable style of living. Her crippled Uncle Willie is forced to spend a night hidden in a vegetable bin, covered with potatoes and onions "like a casserole" because white men, enraged about the supposed insulting of a white woman, are going around indiscriminately beating African-American men. When Maya has a toothache, the local dentist, who has borrowed money from Maya's grandmother, refuses to treat Maya. He says that he would rather "stick my hand in a dog's mouth than in a nigger's" (160).

After the dentist refuses to treat her, Maya dreams of a wild scene of revenge in which her grandmother banishes the dentist from Stamps and he in turn thanks her for not killing him. But these scenes from Maya's imagination, of course, never happen. Her grandmother and her neighbors cannot contest the racism they confront. They are silent, accepting that to try to change the situation would be tantamount to suicide. Thus, after his night of humiliation, Uncle Willie never complains about hiding in the vegetable bin, and Maya's grandmother stands stoically as white children call her by her first name and bare their rear ends to her. In these and other scenes, Maya comes to realize that to survive in Stamps, Arkansas, African-American people must remain silent. This realization plays a significant role in contributing to Maya's sense of powerlessness and her subsequent decision to be silent after she has been raped.

When Maya is nine, her father suddenly appears in Stamps and announces that as soon as he has finished visiting, he is taking Maya and Bailey to their mother in St. Louis. Once again, Maya's life will be disrupted without her consent and once again she will be displaced. To add insult to injury, Maya's father also makes it clear that he prefers his son to his daughter. On the trip north, father and son ignore Maya.

Once all three reach St. Louis, Maya is awestruck by her mother's beauty and her power:

> To describe my mother would be to write about a hurricane in its perfect power. Or the climbing, falling colors of a rainbow . . . My mother's beauty literally assailed me. Her red lips split to show even white teeth and her fresh-butter color looked see-through clean. Her smile widened her mouth beyond her cheeks beyond her ears and seemingly through the walls to the street outside. I was struck dumb.

> I knew immediately why she had sent me away. She was too beautiful to have children. I had never seen a woman as pretty as she who was called "Mother." (49-50)

More damaging than Maya's sense that her mother is "too beautiful to have children" is Maya's sense that her mother, like her father, prefers Bailey to her. Maya is left to watch and feel unwanted and unloved.

Maya's mother (who now goes by the name of Mrs. Baxter) exacerbates Maya's initial feelings of being left out by showing little interest in Maya once she settles into life in St. Louis. Mrs. Baxter is seldom home, but when she is, she makes Maya feel beholden and uncertain about her right to be living under the same roof as a woman as amazing as her mother:

> We each had a room with a two-sheeted bed, plenty to eat and store-bought clothes to wear. And after all, she didn't have to do it. If we got on her nerves or if we were disobedient, she could always send us back to Stamps. The weight of appreciation and the threat, which was never spoken, of a return to [Stamps] were burdens that clogged my childish wits into impassivity. I was called Old Lady and chided for moving and talking like winter's molasses. (57)

Mrs. Baxter's neglectful care for Maya ultimately leads to the most devastating and destructive incident in Maya's childhood: being raped by Mrs. Baxter's lover, Mr. Freeman. As she does with Maya, Mrs. Baxter makes Mr. Freeman feel inferior and insecure. Even Maya recognized that Mr. Freeman was lucky to share a bed with Maya's mother, and he knew his good fortune might not last forever:

> I felt very sorry for Mr. Freeman. I felt as sorry for him as I had felt for a litter of helpless pigs born in our backyard sty in Arkansas. We fattened the pigs all year long for the slaughter on the first frost. (60)

When she arrives in St. Louis, Maya is beset by nightmares and makes a habit of sleeping in the double bed that her mother and Mr. Freeman share. One morning, after Mrs. Baxter has gotten up and gone out, Mr. Freeman forces Maya to hold his penis. He then hugs her with his left hand while he masturbates with his right. While the experience is horrifying to Maya, she finds the aftermath pleasant:

> Finally he was quiet, and then came the nice part. He held me so softly that I wished he wouldn't ever let me go. I felt at home. From the way he was holding me I knew he'd never let me go or let anything bad ever happen to me. This was probably my real father and we had found each other at last. (61)

The pathos is apparent. In her short life, Maya has rarely been hugged. In Arkansas, her Uncle Willie has occasionally held her tightly, her grandmother has held her firmly, and the community of Stamps closed in around her, "[w]armly, but not too familiarly." But no one has held Maya as gently as Mr. Freeman does after he finishes masturbating. She is overwhelmed by the enjoyable physical sensation of the hugging and has no range of experience to help her differentiate between the hug of a father and the hug of a child abuser. Indeed, she assumes that because Mr. Freeman is hugging her, he must be her "real father." Perhaps the most ironic and pathetic element to the passage quoted above is that after Mr. Freeman is finished masturbating, Maya feels "at home."

In many autobiographies of children, the word "home" percolates through the text as children wrestle with what "home" is and should be. For fortunate children, "home" is a place where they are safe and loved by those around them. Maya believes that she is at home when she is in bed with Mr. Freeman.

To silence Maya, Mr. Freeman tells her that if she talks to anyone about what they did in his bed, he will kill Bailey. Fearing for Bailey's life, having no real reason to trust her mother, and not knowing any other adult that she could talk to, Maya remains silent. She thereby makes herself even more vulnerable.

One morning, a few months later, after Maya's mother has failed to come home the night before, Mr. Freeman rapes Maya. His act seems to be as much a way of punishing Maya's mother for her infidelity as it is a way to achieve physical domination of Maya and sexual release. The scene speaks for itself:

> Turning the radio up loud, too loud, he said, If you scream, I'm gonna kill you. And if you tell, I'm gonna kill Bailey." I could tell he

> meant what he said. I couldn't understand why he wanted to kill my brother. Neither of us had done anything to him. And then.
>
> Then there was the pain. A breaking and entering when even the senses are torn apart. The act of rape on an eight-year-old body is a matter of the needle giving because the camel can't. The child gives, because the body can, and the mind of the violator cannot.
>
> I thought I had died—I woke up in a white walled world, and it had to be heaven. But Mr. Freeman was there and he was washing me. (65)

In the aftermath of the rape, Maya's mother finds Maya's bloodied underwear and Mr. Freeman is brought to trial. The trial, however, only further increases Maya's sense of inadequacy, guilt, and self-hatred.

Mr. Freeman's lawyer works to undercut Maya's reliability as a witness and call into question whether Maya was raped. He does so by asking a series of ambiguous questions that forces Maya into answers that destabilize her credibility. The lawyer's success reveals how easily language can be used as a weapon against those who have not mastered it.

Early in the trial, Mr. Freeman's lawyer asks her what Mr. Freeman was wearing. Ostensibly a trivial question—one that could reveal if Maya is truly remembering being raped or imagining it—the question actually creates a no-win situation for Maya. If she remembers what Mr. Freeman was wearing, she will make people wonderer why she should remember what someone was wearing while she was being raped. (Is she infatuated with him, jealous of his love for her mother?) But if, as she does, Maya says she cannot remember what he was wearing, the lawyer can also turn this answer against her:

> "You mean to say this man raped you and you don't know what he was wearing?" He snickered as if I had raped Mr. Freeman. (70)

He then asks her "Do you know if you were raped?" Here again, Maya is caught in a double bind. If she answers yes, he can then cast aspersions on her character, asking the jury what decent eight year old knows what rape is? If she answers no, she undercuts her testimony utterly.

The lawyer continues with his series of double-edged questions. "Was that the first time the accused touched you?" he asks. Again, she is in a bind. If she answers yes, she will savage her credibility (How can a child live in a home for a year and not have been touched by an adult living in that house?) If she answers no, she begs questions about why did she let such touching go on. Maya thinks for a moment and decides that if she admits that Mr. Freeman had touched her before and she had enjoyed some of that experience—she would be admitting a terrible sin and "all the people in the court would stone [her] as they had stoned the harlot in the Bible" (70-71). She tells the court no, Mr. Freeman had never held her before. She knows that the answer is not true and is immediately horrified by her own "dishonesty." She is brought off the stand, inarticulately screaming at Mr. Freeman, "Ole, mean, dirty thing, you. Dirty old thing" (71).

Mr. Freeman is sentenced to a year and a day of jail, revealing that either the jury did not completely believe Maya or did not think that the raping of an eight year old girl was a terribly serious crime. The day after the trial, however, Mr. Freeman is hunted down and beaten to death by Maya's uncles. When Maya hears that Mr. Freeman has been killed, she believes that it was her words, her "lie," that caused his death. She thinks that if she had admitted that Mr. Freeman had held her before, he would not have been judged so harshly.

In short order, Maya, like many children who suffer from physical or sexual abuse, comes to believe that the adult who abused her was "right" and that she was the cause of her own abuse.

> . . . a man had died because I lied. Where was the balance in that? One lie surely wouldn't be worth a man's life. Bailey could have explained it all to me, but I didn't dare ask him. Obviously I had forfeited my place in heaven forever, and I was as gutless as the doll I had ripped to pieces ages ago. Even Christ Himself turned His back on Satan. Would not He turn His back on me? I could feel the evilness flowing through my body and waiting, pent up, to rush off my tongue if I tried to open my mouth. I clamped my teeth shut, I'd hold it in. If it escaped, wouldn't it flood the world and all the innocent people? (72)

Maya decides that the only way she can prevent herself from killing other "innocent" people is if she stops talking:

> In those moments, I decided that although Bailey loved me he couldn't help. I had sold myself to the Devil and there could be no escape. The only thing I could do was to stop talking to people other than Bailey. Instinctively, or somehow, I knew that because I loved him so much I'd never hurt him, but if I talked to anyone else that person might die too. Just my breath, carrying my words out, might poison people and they'd curl up and die like the black fat slugs that only pretended. I had to stop talking. (72-73)

No adult ever tries to explain to Maya what happened or that she did not cause her own rape or Mr. Freeman's death. Instead, the night Mr. Freeman is killed, Grandmother Baxter forbids any further discussion of the incident. Maya's mother never even talks to Maya about the incident. Maya is left to make sense of the events on her own. Maya concludes that she is to blame and she must remain silent. Adults call her silence "impudent," and she is repeatedly "thrashed" for her disrespectfulness. Ultimately, the adults decide to send Maya and Bailey back to Stamps. As usual, no one explains why. And, as usual, Maya concludes that she is at fault for their banishment.

When she arrives back in Stamps, Maya maintains her silence. Bailey impresses all the visitors who come to his grandparents' general store with tall tales about city life up north, but Maya remains sullen and silent. She notices that Uncle Willie watches her all the time, and she fears that he knows about what happened in St. Louis and therefore thinks she is "sinful and dirty." Many clinical psychologists would recognize that she is in a state of deep depression: the sounds she hears are muffled, "as if people are speaking with their hands over their mouths" (75), the colors she sees are muted, she forgets names and cannot remember any details about their accounts at the store. Her mind is preoccupied with the rape, the death of Mr. Freeman, and why she was once again sent away from her mother. Maya remains in this state for more than a year.

Maya Angelou's resurrection from a depressed, self-hating, silent eight year old to a triumphant, self-confident, independent but loved and loving fifteen year old is the story of the last two-thirds of *I Know Why the Caged Bird Sings*. In the first third of her autobiography, Angelou describes the many forces that destroyed her self-confidence, made her vulnerable to Mr. Freeman, and caused her to hate herself and her Blackness. In the last two thirds of *I Know Why the Caged*

Bird Sings, Angelou makes equally clear the forces that rebuilt Maya's self-esteem, re-created her self-confidence and pride, and empowered her to be both loving and loved. Recognizing these positive forces that made her extraordinarily resilient is the focus of the next section of this chapter.

II. BREAKING THE SILENCE AND BUILDING RESILIENCE

A neighbor, Mrs. Bertha Flowers, helps Maya to take the first step out of her depression and silence. Probably at the behest of Maya's grandmother, Mrs. Flowers takes a special interest in Maya. She invites her to her home for tea and cookies and some "lessons in living" (readings and recitations from the works of various authors). To Maya's mind, Bertha Flowers is "the aristocrat of Black Stamps." She has polished speech and manners and acts "just as refined as whitefolks in the movies and books." She makes Maya "proud to be Negro, just by being herself" (79). This pride in being African-American is quite important for Maya, whose sense of racial pride has been severely damaged by the overt racism of the white citizens of Stamps.

In her first conversation with Maya (it is of course mostly a lecture to Maya, since at this point Maya does not speak to anyone except her brother), Mrs. Flowers makes a strong case for Maya to talk again. She tells Maya, "Now no one is going to make you talk—possibly no one can. But bear in mind, language is man's way of communicating with his fellow man and it is language alone which separates him from the lower animals . . . Your grandmother says you read a lot. Every chance you get. That's good, but that's not good enough. Words mean more than what is set down on paper. It takes the human voice to infuse them with the shades of deeper meaning" (82).

The visit and Mrs. Flowers' words makes Maya's spirit soar. At the end of the visit, Maya carefully says good-bye to her benefactor and then runs down the hill toward the store and declares:

> I was liked, and what a difference it made. I was respected not as Mrs. Henderson's grandchild or Bailey's sister but for just being Marguerite Johnson. Childhood's logic never asks to be proved (all conclusions are absolute). I didn't question why Mrs. Flowers had singled me out for attention, nor did it occur to me that Momma might have asked her to give me a little talking to. All I cared about was that she had made tea cookies for *me* and read to *me* from her favorite book. It was enough to prove that she liked me. (85)

In the months to come, Mrs. Flowers continues to pay considerable personal attention to Maya. She repeatedly invites Maya to her home, reads to her, and persistently encourages her to begin speaking again. The impact of Bertha Flowers' efforts is dramatic, significantly strengthening Maya's sense of self and her resolve to speak and break her isolation from the world. Mrs. Flowers' attention causes Maya to see herself as an individual worthy of the interest and concern of an adult who is not a family member and therefore not legally obligated to care for her. Maya feels that she has been sent for, rather than sent away, chosen over Bailey instead of ignored because of him. The impact of this is apparent in *I Know Why the Caged Bird Sings* and is something that Angelou continues to mention in personal interviews some forty years after Bertha Flowers first invited Maya to her home (Elliot 168).

The incidence of non-familial adults helping troubled children is far from unique to Maya Angelou or to the 1930's. Adults who guide and show personal interest in children have been dramatically effective in helping children. A recent study published by The Ford Foundation argues that adult mentors are one of the single most effective way to help troubled children. In *Mentors: Saving America's Children*, Thomas Evans argues that mentors can transform a child's life and revitalize a community and its school system. While I would take issue with much of Evans's book, I agree with him that there are far too few women and men like Bertha Flowers, adults who take special interest in children and give them what is in most short supply these days: time and attention. Most communities, my own included, make role models out of fast-speaking Navy pilots or expensively dressed NBA stars and pay them large fees to appear before hundreds of children and assure them that they, too, can be rich and famous. But after these "role models" speak to the television reporters and pick up their checks, they fly off, having left children with dreams but no support for reaching those dreams. It is good for television news and the annual report of a school system, but it is cruel to children. Bertha Flowers did not fly off after her visit with Maya; she saw her again and again. And thus she had a powerful impact on Maya.

While Mrs. Flowers' care and support help to build Maya's self-esteem and facilitate her breaking of silence, the consistent love and support of Maya's grandmother gives Maya a sense of belonging and self-worth that ultimately empowers her. On first reading, Momma (as Maya calls her grandmother) seems excessively rigid in her beliefs about cleanliness, respect for adults and God, and the general upbringing of children. To be sure, Momma has little patience for tomfoolery or cuddling children. Yet Momma *never* fails in her drive to protect and support and teach her grandchildren. For them, she is always there, perhaps not to sing songs or bake cookies, but always there to protect and nurture. Angelou describes her this way:

> Her world was bordered on all sides with work, duty, religion, and "her place." I don't think she ever knew that a deep-brooding love hung over everything she touched. (47)

If Dr. Alvin Poussaint is right, and the most important thing in the development of a good self-concept in African-American children is consistent care, Momma is most responsible for the development of Maya's increased self-confidence, for she steadfastly provided Maya with consistent care.

In a 1991 edition of *Family Affairs*, Dr. Urie Bronfenbrenner, a Cornell University professor of Human Development widely recognized as the primary designer of the Head Start Program, published an essay that attempts to answer the question "What do successful families do?" Bronfenbrenner's article is lengthy and deserves careful consideration. Nevertheless, I will quote only the first of five propositions that he makes in explaining how families best help children develop successfully. In essense, his point is that a child needs at least one adult who is committed to that child's well-being and development and who is willing to be involved in increasingly complex exchanges of ideas and emotions. Bronfenbrenner writes:

> In order to develop—intellectually, emotionally, socially. and morally—a child requires participation in progressively more complex reciprocal activity, on a regular basis over an extended period in a child's life, with one or more persons with whom the child develops a strong, mutual, irrational emotional attachment and who is committed to the child's well-being and development, preferably for life. (2)

Cutting through his own jargon, Bronfenbrenner explains his phrase "progressively more complex reciprocal activity" by comparing it to a ping-pong game between a parent and a child: "As the partners become familiar with each other, they adapt to each other's style. The game starts to move faster, and the shots in both directions tend to become more complicated, as each player, in effect, challenges the other" (7).

Taking his analogy back into the world of child development, Bronfenbrenner maintains that over the course of hours and days and weeks and months and years of interaction, a child and a parent come not only to understand and respond to each other's simple biological needs but also to each other's far more subtle and sophisticated emotional and psychological needs. This "reciprocal activity" may begin with a parent picking up a child and the two gazing at each other. In time it becomes more complex and includes speaking and all the subtleties of verbal and non-verbal communication. For a child to develop intellectually, emotionally, socially, and morally, Bronfenbrenner argues that there must be an adult who is not only readily and consistently responsive to the communication initiatives of a child over a period of many years but is also able to insure that communication becomes increasingly sophisticated and responsive to the growing and various needs of a maturing child. In addition, the adult must develop a strong emotional attachment to the child and be "committed to the child's well-being and development, preferably for life" (2).

Bronfenbrenner's proposition for child development opens important vistas for understanding *I Know Why the Caged Bird Sings.* In the early years of her life and again in her year in St. Louis, Maya was unable to participate in "progressively more complex reciprocal activity, on a regular basis over an extended period" with her mother or any adult. Maya's mother was either too busy or simply unwilling to do so. (Angelou, in a 1982 interview with Judith Patterson, went so far as to say about her mother, "Well, she was a poor mother for a child. She didn't know what to do with kids, except feed us and things like that" (Elliot 121). Conversely, Maya's grandmother was unquestionably committed to Maya's well-being and development. As noted above, Momma was rigidly autocratic and less likely to be involved in "reciprocal activity" as much as "directed activity" in raising Maya; nevertheless, there is no question that grandmother and granddaughter interacted and communicated on an increasingly sophisticated level over many years. And through all these years, Maya recognized that a "deep brooding love" infused everything her grandmother did.

When my high school and college students have read *I Know the Why the Caged Bird Sings*, they have often been quite critical of Maya's grandmother. They see her as excessively strict and distant. In disagreeing I cite Ann Marsten's excellent article on resilience: "Contributions from the study of children who overcome adversity." Marsten observes that in her study of resilient children, "Parents of [resilient] children at high-risk were less democratic and placed a higher value on self-control than did effective parents of low-risk children. The differences in parenting styles appeared to reflect the rearing context outside the family: a higher level of monitoring and control was probably required to protect children and foster development in the dangerous environment" (429).

Reginald Clark's unique work, *Family Life and School Achievement: Why Poor Black Children Succeed or Fail* makes a slightly different argument, but one that further supports what Maya's grandmother did. In his dissertation-turned-into-book, Clark contends that much research has mistaken descriptive indicators (being poor, being Black, not having a mother and a father) as the causes of failure in school. Clark contends that these researchers have noted that many school dropouts come from poor families and are Black and so they deduce that it is poverty and race that cause children to fail in school. Clark asks that if this is so, how is it that some poor, Black children succeed?

Clark then examines the family life of ten poor, Black, Chicago high school students. Five of the students are "succeeding" in school and five are "failing." What makes this difference? Clark argues that it is the quality and quantity of human interaction in these families—the internal structure and dynamics of home life—that determines whether or not these children succeed. He writes that it is

> . . . family members' *beliefs, activities,* and overall *cultural style,* not the family units' composition or social status, that produces the requisite mental structures for effective and desirable behavior during classroom lessons. (1-2)

Clark goes on to point out that in the homes of the successful children the interpersonal communication patterns

> tended to be marked by frequent parent-child dialogue, strong parental encouragement in academic pursuits, clear and consistent limits set for the young, warm and nurturing interactions, and consistent monitoring of how they used their time. (111)

As one reads Angelou's autobiography—and as the pages to come will try to show—there can be no doubt that Momma provided much of what Clark says distinguishes the homes of successful children. Momma may have provided only modest opportunities for cuddling, but she provided strong parental encouragement in academic pursuits, clear and consistent limits for her interaction with Maya, and exceedingly consistent monitoring of how Maya used her time.

While Momma provides Maya with much of what she needed, it is her brother Bailey that Maya believes is her best friend and the person who loves her most. In a beautiful and important passage early in *I Know Why the Caged Bird Sings*, Angelou writes:

> Bailey was the greatest person in my world. And the fact that he was my brother, my only brother, and I had no sisters to share him with, was such good fortune that it made me want to live a Christian life just to show God that I was grateful. Where I was big, elbowy, and grating, he was small, graceful and smooth. When I was described by our playmates as being shit color, he was lauded for his velvet-black skin. His hair fell down in black curls, and my head was covered with black steel wool and yet he loved me.
>
> . . . . .
>
> Of all the needs (there are none imaginary) a lonely child has, the one that must be satisfied if there is going to be hope and a hope of

> wholeness is the unshaking need for an unshakable God. My pretty Black brother was my Kingdom Come. (17-19)

Maya and Bailey travel through the trials of their lives together, from the first train ride to Stamps to their days in San Francisco. Their allegiance to each other is central to their strength, and Maya realizes that her brother is her most important ally and friend in a frightening world. Most important of all, he is unshakable in his love for her. He defends her against the insults of neighbors and children, he exemplifies an energy of life that she admires, and he loves her.

In "Women's Autobiography and the Male Tradition," the introductory essay for *Women's Autobiography: Essays in Criticism*, Estelle Jelinek contends that in most women's autobiographies there is "an exclusion of siblings." Jelinek goes on to posit that "[a] possible explanation for the absence or near-absence of siblings in most life studies is the fact that most autobiographers are achievers with self-sustaining ego systems . . . " (11). *I Know Why the Caged Bird Sings* obviously does not fit into Jelinek's paradigm, for there is no "exclusion of siblings" in Angelou's work. Bailey is always in the heart of Angelou and *I Know Why the Caged Bird Sings*. Perhaps one way to explain this is to recognize that most of the autobiographies Jelinik uses to support her contention are the life stories of economically privileged white women. These privileged women, unlike Maya Angelou, were not threatened by so many different and very real dangers. Thus, in their protective cocoons of privilege, they could develop their "ego systems" without a sibling's support. It would be hard to underestimate the importance of Bailey.

In the greatest crisis of her childhood, Bailey is Maya's most important support. After she has discovered that Mr. Freeman was beaten to death, Maya decides that she will not speak to anyone *except* to Bailey. This will prevent her from "killing" anyone else:

> The only thing I could do was to stop talking to people other than Bailey. Instinctively, or somehow, I knew that because I loved him so much I'd never hurt him, but if I talked to anyone else that person might die too. (73)

She believes that her love for Bailey is so strong and so pure that it will overcome what she believes is her own innate evil. Thus, their love is even stronger than the "hysterical silencing" caused by the rape. Truly, her "pretty Black brother" is her "Kingdom Come." Until Maya and Bailey return to Stamps and Maya meets with Mrs. Flowers, Maya speaks only to Bailey.

While Momma and Bailey nurture Maya with their love, the Black citizens of Stamps, knowingly and unknowingly, also help to re-build her self-esteem. Throughout her years in Stamps, Maya works in her grandmother's general store. Under her grandmother's vigilant eye, Maya develops full knowledge of what the store sells as well as an uncanny ability to measure and weigh groceries accurately. The store's patrons, essentially the entire African-American community of Stamps, come to appreciate Maya's skills and her honesty. They recognize that she works hard and will not cheat them. They pay her frequent compliments for her excellent work and thereby build her self-esteem. As we have already noted, opportunities for children to demonstrate mastery, whether it be as a Boy Scout, a basketball player, or a store clerk, are critical to the development of children. A community's willingness to provide these opportunities can make a major contribution to the development of resilience in its youth, as Werner and Garmezy have shown.

The African-American citizens of Stamps also organize a wealth of activities that Maya, Bailey, Uncle Willie, and Momma Henderson take part in. Church services, picnics, revivals—these and other occasions bring the African-American community together and give Maya an opportunity to interact with adults, and thereby recognize and appreciate the values and beliefs of the community. These activities also make Maya feel welcome and accepted into a broader community of people. The kind of vicious fighting over status and shades of skin color that is apparent in Anne Moody's autobiography, *Coming of Age in Mississippi*, is nowhere to be found in Angelou's story. The African-American people of Stamps maintain their unity in the face of violence and racism and thus provide for each other and for Maya a sense of group support and fellowship.

In his study of child development, Urie Bronfenbrenner argues that children need the kind of experiences that Maya has with adults outside of her family. Bronfenbrenner contends that experiences that encourage children to interact with adults and do tasks that require thinking are central not only to the social development of children but also to their academic and intellectual development:

> These ongoing experiences remain a potent liberating and energizing force, not only in relation to the physical environment but to the social world as well. Thus they enable the child to relate to persons beyond the immediate family, including peers as well as adults, and to involve them effectively in meeting the child's own developmental needs. At a broader level, the child's newly acquired abilities make it possible to her or him to benefit from experiences in other settings, most notably to learn in school.
>
> In short, the *informal education* that takes place in the family is not merely a pleasant prelude, but rather a powerful prerequisite for success in *formal education* from the primary grades onward. This empowering experience reaches further still. As evidenced in longitudinal studies, it appears to provide a basis, while offering no guarantee, for the subsequent development of the capacity to function responsibly and creatively as an adult in the realms of work, family life, and citizenship. (3)

Research on school dropouts, especially the work conducted by Gary Wehlage, shows that activities with adults are critical to the kind of "social bonding" that adolescents must undergo if they are to join a community of adults. Conversely, other recent research shows that children who do not have these kinds of experiences—children who rarely interact with adults—often do not establish a meaningful bond with adult society and are involved in anti-social and often violent activities. Studies of gang formation and autobiographies such as Sanyika Shakur's *Monster* support this argument.

Stamps schools, while segregated and vastly inferior in resources to the white schools, provide Maya with another opportunity to succeed—and Momma and Uncle Willie insure that Maya takes advantage of this opportunity. From Maya's earliest days, her grandmother and Uncle Willie insist that she do her best work—and all of her work—every day. Maya does as she is told because, as she puts it, she "had the capacity and no alternative" (4). Reginald Clark shows that members of a community can and do make significant contributions to the life of a child. In "Critical Factors in Why Disadvantaged Children Succeed and Fail," Clark writes

> Achievement is best understood as the result of interpersonal communication in everyday life, and this communication occurs in a

> variety of ecological contexts—the home, the school, the neighborhood, and other community institutions . . . " (4)

Clark shows that children who interact with adults and have many opportunities to engage in various learning activities in and out of school are most likely to be successful in school. This should come as little surprise to anyone who has done any research or reading on student academic achievement. The single most consistent variable in determining student success is parental involvement. The work of scholar-practitioners such as Anne Henderson and Joyce Epstein show irrefutably that when parents are engaged in the learning of their children, their children achieve significantly more, whether that is measured by norm referenced standardized tests, grade-point averages, or graduation rates.

The total effect of Momma's guidance, Bailey's love, Uncle Willie's tutoring, the community's compliments, and Mrs. Flowers' mentoring are everywhere apparent when Maya graduates from her junior high school. The ceremony and the days leading up to it demonstrate just how far she has come from being the self-hating silent girl who returned to Stamps after being raped in St. Louis.

To Maya, what is most exciting about the graduation is that she has earned recognition:

> My work alone had awarded me a top place and I was going to be one of the first called in the graduating ceremonies. On the classroom blackboard, as well as on the bulletin board in the auditorium, there were blue stars and white stars and red stars. No absences, no tardinesses, and my academic work was among the best of the year. (145)

Maya receives praise, encouragement, and gifts from many of the people in her community. The minister's wife makes her an underskirt to wear for graduation. Nearly every customer that she waits on in the store gives her a nickel or maybe even a dime with the instruction, "Keep on moving to higher ground," (147). Uncle Willie and Momma give her a Mickey Mouse Watch. Bailey tops that with a beautiful leather bound copy of Edgar Allan Poe poems.

Momma puts her spare time into sewing the butter-yellow pique dress that all the girls are to wear. Having achieved much in school *and* having been recognized for this achievement, Maya now no longer believes that she is physically ugly:

> I was going to be lovely. A walking model of all the various styles of fine hand sewing . . . My hair pleased me too. Gradually the black mass had lengthened and thickened, so that it kept at last to its braided pattern. (144-145)

These emotions are a far cry from the self-deprecating comments Maya makes when she describes herself at the beginning of her story as "a too-big Negro girl, with nappy black hair, broad feet, and a space between her teeth that would hold a number-two pencil" (2). In her dreams, Maya no longer imagines herself as a blond haired white girl but rather as herself, and she sees that self as beautiful.

The actual graduation ceremony begins well but then is nearly ruined by the racist remarks of the school system's white superintendent. He promises the children and the parents that if he is re-elected he will get them a new playing field and equipment for the home economics building and the workshop. Implicitly he reminds them that he wants their education to prepare them to be "maids and farmers, handymen and washerwomen, and anything higher that we aspired to was farcical and presumptuous" (152). Yet the parents and children refuse to let the superintendent have the last words. After he leaves, the class valedictorian delivers his speech and the entire audience, in a show of solidarity and power, joins in singing the "Negro national anthem," James Weldon Johnson's "Lift Ev'ry Voice and Sing." Together, they cleanse away the ugliness that the superintendent left behind. The chapter ends:

> We were on top again. As always, again. We survived. The depths had been icy and dark, but now a bright sun spoke to our souls. I was no longer simply a member of the proud graduating class of 1940; I was a proud member of the wonderful beautiful Negro race. (156)

In sum, the graduation ceremony demonstrates that much of the sorry past of Maya Angelou's childhood is now behind her. Or, as she writes

> Youth and social approval allied themselves with me and we trammeled memories of slights and insults. The wind of our swift passage remodeled my features. Lost tears were pounded to mud and then to dust. Years of withdrawal were brushed aside and left behind, as hanging ropes of parasitic moss. (145)

A few weeks after the graduation ceremony, Maya and Bailey are sent to California to live with their mother. In California, Maya will face many new challenges. But as the final pages of *I Know Why the Caged Bird Sings* show, Maya can now function as an independent self-assured young woman. Maya Angelou, with the help of many, has overcome innumerable obstacles and exemplifies resilience and success.

III. THE VOICE ITSELF

In "Death as Metaphor of Self in *I Know Why the Caged Bird Sings*," Liliane Arensberg argues that death is the prevailing metaphor of the autobiography *and* that death is the "metaphor of self" that best describes Maya Angelou. Arensberg contends that

> [Death] is the metaphor of self which most directly and comprehensively communicates Angelou's identity . . . For, while the book's tone is predominantly witty, even light, resonating just below the surface of almost every page of Angelou's autobiography is the hidden, but everpresent, theme of death. (278)

Arensberg is, I think, exactly wrong. Life is the prevailing metaphor of *I Know Why the Caged Bird Sings*, life and the concomitant joy that is present when, against all odds, a human being triumphs. Angelou's autobiography is full of hope and possibility and vignettes that reveal the potential in even the most threatened and difficult lives.

At a most fundamental level, almost any autobiography is an extended metaphor. Words are symbols and these symbols are used to create and present the "story" of an individual's life. Thus, all autobiographies speak a human triumph. Words have been used to make sense of, make beauty of, make others aware of a life. Of course, these words do not re-create the precise life of the autobiographer;

words can't do that, as a galaxy of deconstructionists have effectively pointed out. But, as James Olney has argued, the words do create a hazy picture, a general sense, a *metaphor*, of the autobiographer's life. Thus, from a "macro" perspective, an autobiography (especially an extraordinary one like *I Know Why the Caged Bird Sings*) testifies to a human triumph, an author's ability to create something significant out of symbols.

Yet beyond the human triumph that autobiography demonstrates, Maya Angelou's particular work—through its descriptive language, metaphors, similes, and sentence structure—testifies to an extraordinary human triumph. Her language, the voice she creates to tell her life story, reveals a virtuosity that makes her autobiography proof of human potential. In many different ways her voice—her word choice, her use of metaphors and similes, her sentence structure, and, most important, her vignettes—at every turn demonstrate an extraordinary triumph of human creativity in the face of disaster. Indeed, it is not just her story but the voice that tells her story that shows that the prevailing metaphor in *I Know Why the Caged Bird Sings* is life, the triumph of life over the many forces of death.

A good place to advance this argument is the opening scene of *I Know Why the Caged Bird Sings*. In this scene, already discussed in the beginning of this chapter, six year old Maya fails to remember the lines she is supposed to recite in front of the congregation of the Colored Methodist Episcopal Church. Deeply embarrassed, she runs out of the church. As she runs, she cannot control her bladder and urine runs down her legs.

It would be hard to underestimate the significance of this scene. It is not only the first scene in *I Know Why the Caged Bird Sings* but it is also one of a small handful of scenes that is achronologic. Throughout her autobiography, Angelou follows a fairly strict chronologic order in recounting her childhood. Yet here, she begins with a description of an experience when she was six and then recommences her story with her first memories at age three. I read the opening scene as a kind of emblematic preface that articulates the prevailing sense of displacement and homelessness apparent throughout much of the first half of Angelou's autobiography. Yet unlike the completely depressing opening scene of Anne Moody's *Coming of Age in Mississippi* or Richard Wright's *Black Boy* or Piri Thomas's *Down These Mean Streets*, Angelou's opening scene offers some cause for hope. Maya escapes from the church and can laugh at the joy she experiences from "being liberated from the silly church." Of course, she understands that she will get a whipping from her grandmother and that her classmates will have something new to tease her about, but she knows, as the scene and the entire autobiography demonstrate, that she can escape.

Just as the scene itself speaks to Maya Angelou's triumph, so too does the language. The voice that describes the scene here, there, and everywhere demonstrates not only a facility with language but virtuosity with the creation of metaphors and similes. There are no fewer than eight similes and three metaphors in the opening two and a half page section. The similes and metaphors present an intriguing balance between Angelou's dreams for the future and her grim reality. She dreams of looking "like a movie star" with a dress that looks "like magic." But her dress makes her skin look "dirty like mud" and her breathing sounds "like crepe paper on the back of hearses." Throughout this scene and throughout *I Know Why the Caged Bird Sings* Angelou plays with metaphors and similes. She is constantly creating them, and thereby not only letting us see something in a different light but also reinforcing the notion that what is could be changed, could be something else. Her dress may make her skin look like mud but it could also look like magic. Inherent in Angelou's use of metaphor is a pervasive sense of possibility, of how things could change, could be different, could be one thing *or* another. Her use of metaphor, thus, destabilizes the generally frightening reality of her world and reminds us that it could be changed, could be different, could be magic or mud.

To read Angelou is to hear and see and smell and taste and feel a world. Looking again at the opening scene, Angelou employs a dozen different colors: a lavender taffeta dress, black Singer sewing machine, black ugly dream, light-blue eyes, long yellow face, green persimmon,—and again they emphasize the possibility (a lavender taffeta dress) and the reality (black ugly dream). If one examines the opening scene of Anne Moody's *Coming of Age in Mississippi* one will see no use of color in the opening passage (save for reference to the master's "white house"). Similarly, in the opening scene of Piri Thomas's *Down These Mean Streets* there is no use of color. In the first chapter of *This Boy's Life* there is only mention of "black smoke" and in *The Woman Warrior* the powerfully visual opening scene is played out with only black, white, and red. Angelou's descriptions remind us of the possibility of beauty in the world. While there is much that is ugly, there is also a possibility of beauty; there is magic and there is mud.

Angelou's sentence structure also emphasizes the potential of life. Using the method of analyzing prose that Richard Lanham develops in his fascinating book *Analyzing Prose,* let's spread the words of the sentences across the page, showing how clauses are related to each other and provide natural pauses. (In the left margin are the numbers of words in each sentence.)

(29) I stumbled and started to say something
or maybe to scream
but a green persimmon
or it could have been a lemon
caught me between the legs and squeezed.

(16) I tasted the sour on my tongue
and felt it in the back of my mouth.

(18) Then before I reached the door
the sting was burning down my legs
and into my Sunday socks.

(66) I tried to hold it
to squeeze it back
to keep it from speeding
but when I reached the church porch
I knew I'd have to let it go
or it would probably run right back
up to my head
and my poor head would burst
like a dropped watermellon
and all the brains and spit and tongue and eyes
would roll all over the place. (3)

The sentences are relatively long throughout the passage (and the autobiography). In this passage, they average 42 words. Thoughts are strung together by conjunctions; look back to the passage above and you will see no fewer than 11 conjunctions. Most show causality, a relationship between one action and another action. Throughout this passage and *I Know Why the Caged Bird Sings*, Angelou uses a polysynechdic style; she links ideas together and shows connectedness. As I will discuss briefly in my chapter on *This Boy's Life*, many contemporary authors, Ernest Hemingway in particular, rarely use connectors. They envision a world of isolated, unconnected people, and consequently, their prose, characters, and plot demonstrate that. I would argue that Angelou, on the other hand, shows connectedness in her prose and her autobiography. Angelou is incorrigibly inclusive, in her prose and her life.

Angelou's polysynechdic style also allows her to establish a rhythm to her prose. Whether one reads *I Know Why the Caged Bird Sings* aloud or listens to Angelou's public readings or taped readings on cassette, it is impossible not to recognize that there is a rhythm, a moving force to what she writes. In part, this rhythm is created by polysynechdic sentence patterns. While Hemingway demands a desultory stop after his short sentences, Angelou's punctuation and connectors discourage you from stopping in the middle of one of her 76 word sentences. Angelou uses rhetorical devises—repetition and chiasmas—to create an internal rhythm. Again, looking at the passage above:

> I tried to hold it
> to squeeze it back
> to keep it from speeding
> but when I reached the church porch
> I knew I'd have to let it go
> or it would probably run right back up to my head
> and my poor head would burst
> like a dropped watermelon,
> and all the brains
> and spit
> and tongue
> and eyes
> would roll all over the place. (3)

The infinitives (to hold, to squeeze, to keep) create a pattern, as do the "its" (hold it, squeeze it, keep it, let it go) and the "ands" (and my poor head, and all the brains, and spit, and tongue, and eyes).

In an interview in which she describes how she writes, Angelou declared, "As a composer writes for musical instruments and a choreographer creates for the body, I search for sound, tempos, and rhythms to ride through the vocal cord over the tongue, and out of the lips of Black people" (Evans 4).

Looking at another passage, just a few pages on in the autobiography, we see the same style. In this section, Angelou is describing her Uncle Willie:

(26) Uncle Willie used to sit
like a giant black Z
(he had been crippled as a child)
and hear us testify
to Lafayette County School's abilities.

(73) His face pulled down on the left side
as if a pulley had been attached to his lower teeth
and his left hand was only a mite bigger
than Bailey's
but on the second mistake
or on the third hesitation
his big overgrown right hand would catch
one of us
behind the collar
and in the same moment would thrust the culprit
toward the dull red heater
which throbbed like a devil's toothache.

(31) We were never burned
although once I might have been
when I was so terrified
I tried to jump on the stove
to remove the possibility
of it remaining a threat.

(22) Like most children, I thought
    if I could face the worst danger voluntarily
        and triumph
    I would forever have power over it.

(10) But in my case of sacrificial effort,
    I was thwarted.

(22) Uncle Willie held tight to my dress
    and I only got close enough to smell
    the clean dry scent
        of hot iron.

(19) We learned the times tables
    without understanding their grand principle
    simply because we had the capacity
        and no alternative.

Again, the sentences are long, averaging more than 30 words. They are littered with connectors, as Angelou again and again shows the relationship between one action and another; hers is a world of connectedness. There is sound, sight, feel, and smell in the passage. There are three similes ("like a giant black Z," "as if a pulley had been attached to his lower teeth", "like a devil's toothache"). The language takes on a strongly religious tenor—Uncle Willie heard Maya "testify," the heater throbs like "the devil's toothache," Maya's effort is "sacrificial." Angelou emphasizes the spiritual aspect of life, the possibility that there is something *more* and different than what is readily apparent.

As I noted in my introductory chapter, Talbott Taylor makes a good point when he argues that a critic's interpretation of "speech events" is "heavily influenced by situational, experiential, emotional, and social factors." (107). Thus, it would not be going too far to argue that my reading of *Caged Bird* as a story, a metaphor, about life and not about death, reveals much about me. What is important to me—as a literary critic, an educational researcher, and a father—is what empowers children, what gives them the ability to overcome obstacles and make life into a fulfilling and joyous experience. In numerous interviews, Angelou has frequently declared her own belief in the possibilities of life. To an interviewer from *Black Scholar* she said:

> Now my problem is I love life, I love living life and I love the art of living, so I try to live my life as a poetic adventure, everything I do from the way I keep my house, cook, make my husband happy, or welcome my friends, raise my son; everything is a part of a large canvas I am creating, I am living beneath.(Elliot 55)

To Stephanie Caruana, Angelou said

> Living life fully, fiercely, devotedly is my goal. It seems to be that life loves the liver. (Elliot 36)

And to Claudia Tate, among others, Angelou has said

> I believe that all things are possible for a human being, and I don't think there's anything I can't do. (Elliot 152)

In her effort to show that death is the prevailing theme of *I Know Why the Caged Bird Sings*, Arensberg examines Maya's graduation from junior high school. While I have discussed this scene above as evidence of Angelou's ultimate triumph over the forces that have tried to silence her, Arensberg sees the scene as evidence of the prevailing metaphor of death in Angelou's work. To prove her point, Arensberg cites Maya's initial reaction to the superintendent's words:

> Then I wished that Gabriel Prosser and Nat Turner had killed all whitefolks in their beds and that Abraham Lincoln had been assassinated before the signing of the Emancipation Proclamation, and that Harriet Tubman had been killed by that blow to the head and Christopher Columbus had drowned in the Santa Maria. It was awful to be Negro and have no control over my life. It was brutal to be young and already trained to sit quietly and listen to charges brought against my color with no chance of defense. We should all be dead. I thought I should like to see us all dead, one on top of the other. A pyramid of flesh with the whitefolks on the bottom, as the broad base, then the Indians with their silly tomahawks and tepees

> and wigwams and treaties, the Negroes with their mops and recipes and cotton sacks and spirituals sticking out of their mouths. (153)

Yet as I've shown above, ultimately Maya's reaction is not one in which death prevails but in which life prevails:

> We were on top again. As always, again. We survived. The depths had been icy and dark, but now a bright sun spoke to our souls. I was no longer a member of the proud graduating class of 1940; I was a proud member of the wonderful, beautiful Negro race. Oh, Black known and unknown poets, how often have your auctioned pains sustained us? Who will compute the lonely nights made less lonely by your songs, or by the empty pots made less tragic by your tales. If we were a people much given to revealing secrets, we might raise monuments and sacrifice to the memories of our poets, but slavery cured us of that weakness. It may be enough, however to have it said that we survive in exact relationship to the dedication of our poets (include preachers, musicians, and blues singers). (156)

Arensberg never examines these final lines.

I Know Why the Caged Bird Sings is an autobiography of triumph. Maya Angelou must travel through a daunting valley littered with an astonishing number of obstacles, yet ultimately she triumphs. Her resilience reflects, of course, her own extraordinary strength. Yet it also testifies to the support given by her family, the adults in her community, and the institutions in Stamps. Maya Angelou's triumph demonstrates that with sufficient support, children can overcome the most profound obstacles.

III
Desperate to be The All-American Boy: *This Boy's Life*

Late in *This Boy's Life*, fifteen year old Tobias Wolff stands in front of a full length mirror in one of Seattle's most exclusive men's clothing stores. He has just been admitted to an elite all-male boarding school and has been brought to the clothing store by a rich alumnus of that school who wants to buy for Toby all the "right clothing." The rich alumnus does not know that Toby earned admission by forging his application, transcript, and letters of recommendation.

Toby, on the other hand, is well aware of how he got into the prep school and even more aware of his mediocre academic record and frequent problems at home and in school. As Toby worries about his future, Toby's benefactor and his wife arrange a claret cashmere scarf over the black cashmere overcoat they have chosen for him. They step back, and Toby is left to look at himself in the mirror:

> The elegant stranger in the glass regarded me with a doubtful, almost haunted expression. Now that he had been called into existence, he seemed to be looking for some sign of what lay in store for him.
>
> He studied me as if I held the answer.
>
> Luckily for him, he was no judge of men. If he had seen the fissures in my character he might have known what he was in for. He might have known that he was headed for all kinds of trouble, and, knowing this, he might have lost heart before the game even got started.
>
> But he saw nothing to alarm him. He took a step forward, stuck his hands in his pockets, threw back his shoulders and cocked his head. There was a dash of swagger in his pose, something of the stage cavalier, but his smile was friendly and hopeful. (275-276)

The dichotomy between the speaker and the image in the mirror is dramatic and revealing. For Toby, the image in the mirror is the embodiment of what he has always wanted to be—a self-assured, independent, all-American boy. Yet Toby knows that he is not the elegant stranger in the mirror, but rather the mirror image of that figure. He is very thankful that the boy in the mirror and his benefactor are "no judge of men" and cannot see "the fissures in his character." If they could, he believes that they would surely abandon him.

I begin my discussion of *This Boy's Life* with a description of this scene because I believe it speaks to the central issues of Tobias Wolff's childhood—his deep desire to be the all-American boy and his profound sense of inadequacy because he feels he is not that boy. Throughout *This Boy's Life*, Toby struggles to demonstrate his masculinity, be the stage cavalier, and act the tough and independent boy that American culture idealizes. Yet no matter what Toby does, he always knows that he does not measure up to the rigid specifications of the all-American boy. In part, Toby's pervading sense of inadequacy can be blamed on the unobtainable nature of the mythic all-American boy. However, Toby's sense of personal failing must be more substantially blamed on a half dozen different men who mistreat him and savage his confidence throughout his youth.

Toby is repeatedly rejected and humiliated by men who cross his path. After his mother separates from his father, Toby does not receive even so much as a letter from his father for ten years. His mother's subsequent companions and her second husband belittle and abuse Toby in some of the cruelest ways imaginable. In a sense, *This Boy's Life* is not only a chronicle of the pressures that American boys feel as they attempt to live up to the American ideal of boyhood but also a chronicle of the damage that men can inflict on boys and, more specifically, that fathers can inflict on their sons.

Yet, despite all its sadness and poignancy, *This Boy's Life* ultimately testifies to the resilience of children and the enormous power and importance that a mother's support can provide. Because of his own intelligence and resilience, the unconditional love and support of his mother, and, ultimately, his ability to describe, in writing, who he wants to be and how he wants to live, Tobias Wolff escapes a grim childhood and lives not only to write about it but to live and love well.

I. DESPERATE TO BE THE ALL-AMERICAN BOY

Tobias Wolff begins his childhood autobiography by remembering how when he was seven, his mother separated from Toby's philandering father and took him, the youngest of her two sons, on a drive west to start a new life. Like generations of 19th century Americans, they are going west to strike it rich, not with gold in California, but with newly prized uranium in Utah. And while they dream of striking it rich, they also dream of taking on new identities, transforming themselves into the people that they want to be. Toby, although only seven, wants to become a "new man."

The second chapter of his autobiography begins with this reminiscence of their first days in their new home state of Utah:

> I didn't come to Utah to be the same boy I'd been before. I had my own dreams of transformation. Western dreams, dreams of freedom and dominion and taciturn self-sufficiency. The first thing I wanted to do was to change my name. A girl named Toby had joined my class before I left Florida, and this had caused both of us scalding humiliation.
>
> I wanted to call myself Jack, after Jack London. I believed that having his name would charge me with some of the strength and competence inherent in my idea of him. The odds were good that I'd never have to share a classroom with a girl name Jack. (8)

This passage is rich with Toby's desire to become the all-American boy, full of the values that "real men" possess. He dreams of "freedom" and "dominion." He wants to be self-sufficient and taciturn, a combination of Jack Armstrong and Jack London.

Feminist critic Nina Baym has argued that the commonly accepted canon of American literature revolves around "melodramas of beset manhood," overwrought stories about men leaving civilization and striking out for a new unsettled land where they can live an unfettered life and become the ideal men they want to be, free from society's conventions and women's demands (63-80). Since Toby is traveling with his mother, his journey west cannot be an exact re-enactment of this paradigm. Nevertheless, the qualities Toby wants "freedom," "taciturn self-sufficiency," and "dominion" are exactly the qualities that Baym points out that Natty Bumpo and Huck Finn and Ishmael search for and that are typically seen as quintessentially male.

Moreover, Toby does not want to be mistaken for a girl. The *first* thing he wants to do is change his name. He wants to be Jack because it sounds strong and male and because it reminds him of Jack London (another author who champions men going off into the womanless wilderness and proving their courage, self-sufficiency, and power). Toby hopes that a new name will give him strength and competence, qualities that he believes will help him demonstrate his masculinity and put to rest any questions about why he ended up with his mother and not his father.

Toby worries constantly about his masculinity. Why did his father choose to let Toby go with his mother yet keep Toby's older brother, Geoffrey? Why did Toby want to stay with his mother? Is he a "momma's boy?" Although his mother agrees to let him change his name, throughout most of his childhood Toby struggles to take on not just the name but to act the part of a Jack. Again and again, *This Boy's Life* describes Toby's endless attempts to act as he thinks men should act.

After he and his mother settle in Salt Lake City, Toby decides that more than anything he wants a gun. He believes that a gun will make him independent and whole: "A weapon was the first condition of self-sufficiency, and of being a real Westerner, and of all acceptable employment—trapping, riding herd, soldiering, law enforcement and outlawry. I needed that rifle, for itself and for the way it completed me when I held it" (23).

Toby's mother lets her son have a gun and in short order he begins to use it to enact fantasies of domination over neighbors and imaginary soldiers. First, Toby marches around the apartment like a soldier, then he strikes brave poses in front of the mirror, and finally he pretends that he is a sniper and spends hours at his apartment window aiming a loaded gun at unsuspecting passers-by. He revels in the feeling of power this gives him:

> Hammer cocked, a round in the chamber, finger resting lightly on the trigger, I drew a bead on whoever walked by—women pushing strollers, children, garbage collectors laughing and calling to each other, anyone—and as they passed under my window I sometimes

> had to bite my lip to keep from laughing in ecstasy of my power over them, and their absurd and innocent belief that they were safe. (25)

Toby's need for power and control is palpable here, reflecting his sense of a lack of control over his own life while he lives in Salt Lake City. He and his mother move from apartment to apartment, unconnected to the rest of their family and apart from the strong family and religious structure of the dominant Mormon community.

Toby spends much of his time in Utah feeling deeply inadequate and at fault for not having a father and not having a "respectable" home:

> I was subject to fits of feeling myself unworthy, somehow deeply at fault. It didn't take much to bring this sensation to life, along with the certainty that everybody but my mother saw through me and did not like what they saw. (11-12)

In a particularly poignant scene of his first confession, Toby feels so guilty that he cannot even begin to confess:

> I thought about what to confess, but I could not break my sense of being at fault down to its components. Trying to get a particular sin out of it was like fishing a swamp, where you feel the tug of something that at first seems promising and then resistant and finally hopeless as you realize that you've snagged the bottom, that you have the whole planet on the other end of your line. (17)

Such a deeply felt sense of guilt and inadequacy is not uncommon to children of divorced or separated parents. As we'll explore more fully in the final chapter, Debra Mullholland, Norman Watt, Emmy Werner, Robert Blakeslee, and Thomas Wallerstein have all shown that children commonly assume that it is their failings and misbehavior that caused parents to separate; the damage from this guilt often endures throughout childhood and into adulthood.

In her study of 60 children of divorce, Debra Mulholland shows that children of divorce typically experience considerable pain and difficulties. Their experiences often include receiving lower grades in school, having a persistent and long term lack of motivation in school and at home, fewer friends, and less involvement in activities and social events. Moreover, Mulholland finds that "at least some children of divorce experience residual effects insidiously over many years . . . [divorce] acts like a slow virus . . . and that the acute disturbances that erupt at the onset of parental divorce, although not easily dismissed, are relatively benign in contrast with the longer term, insidious but potent effects that dampen the vitality and enthusiasm of children and jaundice their outlook on life" (278-279).

The full impact of his parents' separation is unknowable, of course, but surely some of Toby's sense of guilt and his obsession to prove his masculinity stem from being separated from and rejected by his own father. When Toby's parents decided that their marriage had to end, Toby's older brother, Geoffrey, stayed with his father and Toby went with his mother. In a moving and telling scene, Toby recalls some early days in Utah that he spent searching for his father and pretending that indeed he found him. The scene Toby provides is Freudian, in simplest terms a search for a father:

> Most afternoons I wandered around in the trance that habitual solitude induces. I walked downtown and stared at merchandise. I imagined being adopted by different people I saw on the street. Sometimes, seeing a man in a suit come toward me from a distance that blurred his features, I would prepare myself to meet my father and to be recognized by him. Then we would pass each other and a few minutes later I would pick someone else. (12)

Toby's desire to be recognized and accepted by his father is apparent throughout his autobiography. Moreover, for most of his autobiography, Toby makes few critical comments about his father. Toby imagines him as an ideal man, a perfect father, and never questions why he never writes or calls or visits. Instead, he spends his time wondering what he did that made him so expendable to his own father.

Interestingly, Geoffrey Wolff, Tobias Wolff's brother, has written his own childhood autobiography, one that focuses primarily on his relationship with their father. *The Duke of Deception: Memories of My Father* is a sad story. Geoffrey poignantly recounts his youth, continually and at times uncharitably describing the many failings of his father. Geoffrey and Tobias's father was a man whose life was a web of deception, full of lies about his education and employment, tastes and experiences.

Early in *The Duke of Deception*, in one of only a handful of references to Toby, Geoffrey indicates that he stayed with his father and Toby went with his mother because of their personalities. Geoffrey was more aggressive and outgoing, like his father, while Toby was smaller, quieter, and more like his mother. In *The Duke of Deception*, Geoffrey recalls that after a stomach operation, Toby became "fussy and spoiled" and took

> advantage of an absolute injunction against hitting or pushing him, and my mother took his side in our disputes: [Toby] was endangered in a way I was not, he was littler, and he resembled [my mother] in appearance and temperament as I resembled my father. Greater distance opened between us. I would swear that [my father] did nothing to divide my mother from me, that he never suggested that she wasn't brilliant or that her taste wasn't flawless. Yet my mother felt his judgment on her like a weight, and if memory is false, perhaps she and I were nudged, and did not merely drift, apart. (107)

Whether Toby's father did or did not side with Geoffrey is perhaps a moot point. What Toby remembers is what counts, and Toby remembers feeling a sense of being rejected by his father.

While Toby rarely criticizes his father, there is a powerful passage in the middle of *This Boy's Life* in which Tobias Wolff breaks the chronology of the story of his childhood and reveals just how much damage his father did to him. This passage comes at a point where Toby and Rosemary are living in Chinook, Washington with a man named Dwight, whom Rosemary married in an attempt to provide Toby with a father. The marriage turns out miserably, and Dwight verbally and physically abuses Toby. At the point of the passage, Toby is remembering how and why he missed his real father:

> [My real father] had the advantage always enjoyed by the inconstant parent, of not being there to be found imperfect. I could see him as I wanted to see him. I could give him sterling qualities and imagine good reasons, even romantic reasons, why he had taken no interest, why he had never written to me, why he seemed to have forgotten I

> existed. I made excuses for him long after I should have known better. (121)

Toby's words echo Maya Angelou's words after she and her brother Bailey receive Christmas gifts from their parents, whom they have not seen in years:

> The gifts opened the door to questions that neither of us wanted to ask. Why did they send us away? and What did we do so wrong? So Wrong? Why, at three and four, did we have tags put on our arms to be sent by train alone from Long Beach, California to Stamps, Arkansas, with only the porter to look after us? (43)

Why? Why? Why? the children ask. And then Wolff breaks the chronology of his story and reveals that long after his childhood he realized not only how naive he had been in his sympathetic judgement of his father but also just how much his father had hurt him:

> This way of thinking [that his father was perfect and had good reasons for not paying his son any attention] worked pretty well until my first child was born. He came three weeks early, when I was away from home. The first time I saw him, in the hospital nursery, a nurse was trying to take a blood sample from him . . . When I finally got my hands on him I felt as if I had snatched him from a pack of wolves, and as I held him something hard broke in me, and I knew that I was more alive than I had been before. But at the same time I felt a shadow, a coldness at the edges. It made me uneasy, so I ignored it. I didn't understand what it was until it came upon me again that night, so sharply I wanted to cry out. It was about my father, ten years dead by then. It was grief and rage, mostly rage, and for days I shook with it when I wasn't shaking with joy for my son, and for the new life I had been given. (121-122)

As he holds his first born child—a moment that for myself was the single most exhilarating experience of my life, save for my marriage ceremony—Tobias Wolff feels joy and awe but also the pain of his father's rejection.

While Toby's father wounds him, so too do virtually all the other men that Rosemary meets during Toby's childhood. In Utah,

Rosemary and Toby live with Roy, a pathetic ne'er do well who has chased Rosemary across the country. Roy does not work; he has a small inheritance and receives disability checks that give him a reason not to look for a job. He spends his days fishing and hunting and reading *The Shooter's Bible.* Roy is so insecure that every afternoon when Rosemary's job as a secretary is over, he gets in his Jeep and shadows her home to make sure that she is not being unfaithful to him. When she won't do exactly what he wants, he whines. And when that doesn't work, he hits her.

Toby does not know the specifics of what Roy does to his mother, but he understands that Roy hurts her:

> My mother didn't tell me what went on between her and Roy, the threats and occasional brutality with which he held her in place . . . Only now and then there came a night when she couldn't do anything but sit and cry, and then I comforted her, but I never knew the reasons. (14)

Perhaps because he sees that his mother chooses to live with Roy, or perhaps because he sees no other better male role models, Toby assumes that Roy is "what a man should be:"

> Roy was handsome in the conventional way that appeals to boys. He had a tattoo. He'd been to war and kept a kind of silence about it that was full of heroic implications. He was graceful in his movements. He could fix the Jeep if he had to, though he preferred to drive halfway across Utah to a mechanic he'd heard about from some loudmouth in a bar. He was an expert hunter who always got his buck. (14)

Rosemary's relationship with Roy sends Toby all sorts of mixed messages of what a man should be. Toby sees that the man his mother chooses to live with is violent and lazy, that somehow being ruggedly handsome and having a tattoo, military experience, and the ability to fix a jeep and shoot a buck are acceptable qualifications to win the affection of his mother.

Luckily for Toby, when Roy starts to talk about having a family, Rosemary starts packing. She and Toby leave without even saying goodbye to Roy. They take a bus to Seattle, but here Rosemary only finds more abusive men. Her first encounter is at SeaFair, a public carnival on Seattle's waterfront. She meets two men who win her attention by ingratiating themselves with Toby. They offer him lunch and a bicycle, and Rosemary subsequently accepts an invitation to dinner with the older member of the duo. What happens on the date is not entirely clear, but the implication is that Rosemary's date tries to force her to have intercourse.

Her fortunes get no better. Rosemary begins to date another man, named Dwight. He lives three hours north of Seattle in a company town called Chinook. Although he too is pathetic—a liar and a tyrant—Rosemary considers his marriage proposal because she so wants Toby to have a father. But before she accepts Dwight's proposal, Rosemary arranges for Toby to move to Chinook and live with Dwight and his three children for a trial run.

From his very first day in Chinook, Toby is abused by Dwight. Having heard from one of Rosemary's friends that Toby imitates him, Dwight roughs up Toby the first night he is in Chinook. Every night thereafter, Dwight requires him to spend at least an hour tending to a fiendishly useless task—husking horsechestnuts. He arranges for Toby to take on the town's paper route but keeps every penny of Toby's pay. He gives Toby orders every day and punishes him for the slightest transgressions. And he makes an in-depth study of Toby's shortcomings:

> Dwight made a study of me. He thought about me during the day while he grunted over the engines of trucks and generators, and in the evening while he watched me eat, and late at night while he sat heavy-lidded at the kitchen table with a pint of Old Crow and a package of Camels to support him in his deliberations. He shared his findings as they came to him. The trouble with me was, I thought I was going to get through life without doing any work. The trouble with me was, I thought I was smarter than everyone else. The trouble with me was, I thought other people couldn't tell what I was thinking. The trouble with me was, I didn't think. (95)

But ultimately when Rosemary asks Toby if she should marry Dwight, Toby tells her to go ahead. He cannot articulate how badly he has been treated. In part, his silence stems from his deeply held belief that he is at fault; like his initial attempt at confession, he believes that he is the cause and he deserves his situation:

> I had come to feel that all of this was fated, that I was bound to accept as my home a place I did not feel at home in, and to take as my father a man who was offended by my existence and would never stop questioning my right to it. I did not believe my mother when she told me it wasn't too late. (104)

Consequently, Rosemary accepts Dwight's proposal and moves to Chinook, but their marriage is almost immediately nightmarish. Their Vancouver honeymoon ends prematurely and when they return they are not speaking. In the weeks that follow, Dwight verbally and physically abuses Rosemary and constantly complains about the cost of raising Toby. Most nights, Dwight gets drunk and on more than one occasion ends up hitting Toby.

Modeling the behavior of Dwight and Roy, Toby gets himself into fist fights. His first fight is with Arthur, a boy who is actually a good friend. After the fight, Toby finds that Dwight is not angry at him but impressed and gleefully tells neighbors that "his boy" gave another boy a shiner. A year later, Toby gets into another fight with Arthur and, since the fight took place at school, their school's shop teacher demands that the two boys make their argument part of a school sponsored "smoker," an evening of boxing matches between the boys in the high school. Tickets cost three dollars and sell out in a matter of days. Dwight, of course, is delighted and pays Toby more attention in the days before the fight than ever before.

The fight itself is a horrendous display of rabid parents and roundhouse punches. For the most part, Toby takes a pretty bad beating, but he does land one or two punches. When he does hit Arthur, Toby feels something he has never felt before: a bond of love between himself and Dwight:

> I caught [Arthur] with that uppercut twice more during the final round, but neither of them rocked him like that first one. That first one was a beaut. I launched it from my toes and put everything I had into it, and it shivered his timbers. I could feel it travel through him in one pure line. I could feel it hurt him. And when it landed, and my old friend's head snapped back so terribly, I felt a surge of pride

> and connection; connection not to him but to Dwight. I was distinctly aware of Dwight in that bellowing mass all around me. I could feel his exultation at the blow I'd struck, feel his own pride in it, see him smiling down at me with recognition and pleasure, and something like love. (221)

Toby feels his step-father's "exultation" and "something like love" when he hits another boy. This explicit connection between love and violence and father and son is central to an understanding of the forces that shape Tobias Wolff's childhood. The ritualization of the violence—and the community's support of it—also explain something of what this boy's life was really like.

While the community of Chinook offers Toby very little of the kind of varied and extraordinary support that Stamps provided Maya Angelou, the community's local Boy Scout Troop did provide Toby with recreation, some friends, and some opportunities to demonstrate skills and mastery. Scouting gives him a chance to make friends and earn the respect of other boys and men. Scouting also offers him the opportunity to learn the skills of independent frontiersmen, manly skills such as rope craft, hiking, camping, cooking without utensils.

In her path-breaking work on the development of self-esteem in children, Edith Jacobson has shown that a child's self-esteem is in large part developed through "the experience by the child of real accomplishment, the pleasure or satisfaction in successful mastery of tasks or activities he or she has initiated. The experience of being effective or competent in areas the child designates as important to his or her self-concept, whether physical attraction, athletics, intellectual achievement or popularity with peers, will contribute strongly to positive self-regard" (Mack and Hickler 103). As Jacobson argues most children do, Toby enjoys the sense of mastery that he gets from Boy Scouting and the cloth merit badges that he gets. He marvels at the status that the badges and their concomitant ranks give him and quickly develops "a headwaiter's eye" in order to read the uniforms of other scouts and see who has what status.

But perhaps most of all, Toby enjoys Boy Scouting because it allows him to participate in his fantasy of becoming the ideal boy that Boy Scouting—and American culture—promote: "But I liked being a scout. I was stirred by the elevated diction in which we swore our fealty to the chaste chivalric fantasies of Lord Baden-Powell" (102).

He reads the Scout *Handbook* and likes its voice, "the bluff hail-fellow language by which it tried to make being a good boy seem adventurous, even romantic." Toby especially enjoys reading the official publication of Boy Scouting, the magazine *Boys' Life*:

> I read it in a trance, accepting without question its narcotic invitation to believe that I was really no different from the boys whose hustle and pluck it celebrated. Boys who raised treasure from Spanish galleons, and put empty barns to use by building operational airplanes in them. Boys who skied to the North Pole. Boys who sailed around the Horn, solo. Boys who saved lives, and were accepted into savage tribes, and sent themselves to college by running traplines in the wilderness. (103-104)

One needs only to browse through a few copies of 1950's *Boys' Life* to recognize the "narcotic invitation" the magazine could offer to a boy wanting to be a "real boy." The magazine is filled with adventure stories and columns on skills and hobbies (model railroading and magic tricks, cooking without utensils and hiking by the stars). As he reads *Boys' Life*, Toby can dream about (and feel a part of) this idealized world of independent, self-sufficient, rugged boys.

Wolff's description of *Boys' Life* as something that celebrates boys with "hustle and pluck" calls to mind Horatio Alger's boys who use a little bit of luck and pluck to become American success stories. And while Wolff's allusion to Alger is relevant here, Wolff's own allusion to *Boys' Life* is even more relevant. Tobias Wolff entitles his childhood autobiography *This Boy's Life*—and in so doing he calls to mind the differences between his life, chronicled in *This Boy's Life*, and the idealized world of boys featured in *Boys' Life*. Wolff's title reminds us that his life was not in any way like that of the boys featured in the official publication of Boy Scouting. That is *Boys' Life* and he is telling us a different story, the story of *this* boy's life. The difference of those two worlds is at the heart of Wolff's work.

There is, I am told, another allusion in Wolff's title, this one to Edmund White's quasi-fictional, quasi-autobiographical work, *A Boy's Own Story*. While White's novel is primarily concerned with the main character's homosexuality, *A Boy's Own Story* and *This Boy's Life* both consider very carefully the notion of masculinity, relationships between fathers and sons, men and boys. After *This Boy's Life* was published, Edmund White received a letter from Tobias Wolff in which Wolff thanked White and acknowledged that *A Boy's Own Story* was much in his mind while writing *This Boy's Life*.

Toby's fascination with Boy Scouting reflects his deep desire to demonstrate and possess the qualities he believes will prove his masculinity. At all costs, he wants to avoid being perceived as a sissy. While he is in Boy Scouts, Arthur, the boy he fought in the school sponsored "smoker," becomes his best friend. Arthur is bright, sensitive, and, like Toby, very lonely. But Arthur is also un-athletic and unwilling to try to play the part of the all-American boy. Toby never allows himself to be perceived as Arthur's best friend for fear of the two being labeled queer. Yet the two boys spend a great deal of time together, and at one point they kiss each other. But whenever he is away from Arthur, Toby makes a point of belittling Arthur and telling other boys that Arthur is a sissy.

Toby is convinced that he must choose between being a man or being a sissy, being a boy scout or being a friend of Arthur. He visualizes masculinity as an "either/or proposition" and at all turns he makes decisions that he believes are in harmony with being a man. In her book *Woman Hating*, Andrea Dworkin argues convincingly that the notion of sexual absolutes is both ridiculous and dangerous:

> The discovery is, of course, that "man" and "woman" are fictions, caricatures, cultural constructs. As models they are reductive, totalitarian, inappropriate to human becoming. As roles they are static, demeaning to the female, dead-ended for male and female both . . .
>
> We are, clearly, a multisexed species which has its sexuality spread along a vast continuum where the elements called male and female are not discrete. (183)

For Toby, however, his world view is of absolutes. He is obsessed with the desire to be "male" and not "female."

As Toby gets older, he comes to blows with his Dwight more and more frequently, sometimes over things as significant as telling lies and sometime over things as trivial as not getting all the mustard out of a mustard jar. Finally, the violence between the two of them is too much for Rosemary, and she arranges for Toby to live with another family. As Toby is leaving, he shakes hands with Dwight but realizes that their banal wishes for "good luck" are insincere:

> We hated each other. We hated each other so much that other feelings didn't get enough light. It disfigured me. When I think of Chinook I have to search for the faces of my friends, their voices, the rooms where I was made welcome. But I can always see Dwight's face and hear his voice. I hear his voice in my own when I speak to my children in anger. They hear it too, and look at me in surprise. My youngest once said, "Don't you love me anymore?" (233)

In this passage, as he does in the passage about the birth of his first child, Tobias Wolff breaks the chronology of his autobiography and projects the reader into the present. As before, this technique draws attention to the point he is making and lends weight to his observation. We hear an adult speaking about the present (not an adult trying to remember the past) and we recognize just how long that emotion has survived. The hatred between Toby and Dwight is the defining element in their relationship and, indeed, in any discussion of the obstacles Toby faced in his childhood.

The battle between fathers and sons is central to many autobiographies of boys, including Piri Thomas's *Down These Mean Streets*, Claude Brown's *Manchild in the Promised Land*, Richard Wright's *Black Boy*, and John Edgar Wideman's *Brothers and Keepers*. Edmund White's autobiographical novel, *A Boy's Own Story*, also revolves around a son's conflict with his father. These works and *This Boy's Life* offer evidence to support the rather obvious—but important not to overlook—idea that conflict between a father and a son helps to create a desperate childhood for many boys. Certainly, Toby's sense of rejection by his own father and horrendous relationship with his step-father made his childhood miserable.

II. A MOTHER'S UNCONDITIONAL LOVE

Yet if Dwight, Roy, and Toby's biological father as well as the cultural script of the all-American boy put Toby at great risk, his mother's unconditional love provides the constancy and support that he so desperately needs. As Geoffrey Wolff's work implies, Toby and

Rosemary are very close from their earliest days. Throughout *This Boy's Life*, Toby's profound love for his mother is everywhere apparent. She, in turn, steadfastly supports and defends him.

When their Seattle roommates point out Toby's misdeeds and failings, Rosemary argues that it is just a phase he is going through. When Toby gets caught writing an obscenity on the school's bathroom wall, Rosemary refuses to accept Toby's guilt and bullies the principal into giving him no punishment. When Dwight criticizes Toby, Rosemary defends him.

Nowhere is the strength of the bond between mother and son more apparent than when Toby is offered a chance to move to Paris and live with his uncle. After having sent his uncle an embellished account of how tough their life is with Dwight in Chinook, Toby receives, by return mail, an invitation from his uncle to leave Dwight and Chinook behind. But as the terms of his uncle's offer unfold, Toby realizes that if he moves to Paris, he will not only have to leave his mother behind but also agree to be adopted by his aunt and uncle and become, legally, their son. Toby decides that this is too high a price to pay:

> Whenever I was told to think about [going to Paris], my mind became a desert. By this time, I had no need of thought, because the answer was already there. *I was my mother's son. I could not be anyone else's*. When I was younger and having trouble learning to write, she sat me down at the kitchen table and covered my hand with hers and moved it through the alphabet for several nights running, and then through words and sentences until the motions assumed their own life, partly hers and partly mine. I could not, cannot, put pen to paper without having her with me. Nor swim, nor sing. I could imagine leaving her. I knew I would, someday. But to call someone else my mother was impossible. (142, emphasis mine)

Tobias Wolff realizes that, no matter what, he is his mother's son—and can be no one else's. She is part of everything he does and part of everything he writes. And Tobias Wolff is a writer. Examining the scene he chooses to use to explain their closeness, we see that she metaphorically, emotionally, and physically helps him become a writer. They join hands around a pen and write. If we project the implications of the passage to the present, we realize that indeed, she is, quite literally, part of what he has just written and we have just read. This is her text as well as his.

In "'The Blank Page' and The Issues of Female Creativity," Susan Gubar has shown that there is a long tradition of literature that identifies "the author as a male who is primary and generative and the female as his passive creation—a secondary object lacking autonomy, endowed with often contradictory meaning but denied intentionality" (295). Gubar proffers a metaphor of a pen (representing the male penis) writing on a blank page (the virgin female). Gubar shows that such a paradigm is useful in the analysis of "The Blank Page" and other works, and I believe that it can be reworked to shed light on *This Boy's Life. Toby's initial* writing is controlled by Rosemary; the pen-penis is directed by her until the motions of the pen-penis "assumed their own life, *partly hers and partly mine*." After Toby has mastered the physical act of writing, her influence is not solely limited to the initial task-specific neuro-muscular training that she has given him. Toby finds that he "could not, cannot, put pen to paper without having her with me." The use of the present tense "cannot" is significant. Even as Tobias writes his life story, Rosemary is with him. This is his story, but it is also their story.

Of course, their bond was not always healthy for Toby. At times, he is so close to his mother that he stops being a son and sees himself as her protector and a partner who becomes jealous when other men try to court her. When Toby and Rosemary leave Roy and Utah, Toby is glad because he will "have her to myself again." When Rosemary begins to date Dwight, Toby acknowledges that he examined Dwight with "the eye of a competitor" and decides that he needn't worry about Dwight joining them because of his defects: "We hadn't come all the way out here to end up with him" (63).

In *Refusing To Be A Man*, John Stoltenberg argues that many fathers desire to win their sons back from their mothers, essentially to assert their paternal rite of domination over their children. Stoltenberg contends that one way that fathers win back their sons is by brutalizing the mother and thus showing the son his ultimate fate if he does not re-join the father's side. Because I want to spend some time examining Stoltenberg's argument in discussing Toby's relationship with his mother and his surrogate fathers, I will take the liberty of reproducing a long excerpt from one of Stoltenberg's essays:

> The father's struggle to repossess the son will be played out in front of the boy's uncomprehending eyes and upon the bodies of both the boy and the mother. Of course, the father will be aided and abetted by schools, television, and other cultural accessories to the theft of sons from mothers. But the father figure in the flesh will succeed in dividing the boy's eroticism against the mother only by physical or emotional brutality. The boy will be a witness as the father abuses his wife—once or a hundred times, it only needs to happen once, and the boy will be filled with fear and helpless to intercede. Then the father will visit his anger upon the boy himself, uncontrollable rage, wrath that seems to come from nowhere, punishment out of proportion to any infraction of any rules the boy knew existed—once or a hundred times, it only needs to happen once, and the boy will wonder in agony why the mother did not prevent it. From that point onward, the boy's trust in the mother decays, and the son will belong to the father for the rest of his natural life.
>
> The authority of the anger of the father is interpreted by the son as follows: (1) Not-mother hates Mother and Not-mother hates me; Not-mother hates us. (2) It is because I am like Mother that Not-mother hates me so. (3) I should be different from Mother; the more different I am from Mother, the safer I will be. These are the cardinal principles of logic in male maturation under father right. They are so simple, even a child can understand. They are backed up by the constant threat of the father's anger, so the child will remember them, and the child will never forget.
>
> The son, in order to become as different from Mother as he can possibly be, now begins to rid his body of the eroticism of the mother. He withdraws from it. He purges it with aggression. (72-73)

Stoltenberg's analysis of the impact of paternalism and a father's brutality towards his wife offers several useful insights to understanding Toby's behavior. First, it is clear that in Utah and in Washington, Toby lives in fear of offending his (surrogate) father. He understands the physical danger such behavior will create for him. Dwight hits him often. And Toby recognizes that when he is physically abusive, when he beats on Arthur or any other boy, he earns his father's respect and "something like love." In short, he recognizes that the more he behaves in a way that his father deems acceptable, the less likely he is to be physically and verbally abused. Yet, ultimately

Stoltenberg's paradigm does not satisfactorily explain Toby's behavior or *This Boy's Life*. Stoltenberg argues that after a son has witnessed the wrath of his father on his mother, "the boy's trust in his mother decays, and the son will belong to the father for the rest of his natural life." While Toby's behavior parallels some of what Stoltenberg believes it should, Toby's trust in his mother never diminishes. Throughout *This Boy's Life* Toby's love for his mother is everywhere apparent. He refuses to go to Paris because he can only be his mother's son.

Stoltenberg's paradigm fails because it is, like much of his book, unbalanced. Too often, Stoltenberg sees all men as violent ogres whose deepest desire is to repopulate the world with miniature versions of their violent selves. Stoltenberg creates an absolutist world view that makes for interesting reading but ultimately an unbalanced argument. For example, Stoltenberg argues that "a fully realized male sexual identity also requires *non-identification with* that which is perceived to be nonmale, or female. His identity as a member of the sex class men absolutely depends on the extent to which he repudiates the values and interests of the sex class "women" (34). Stoltenberg argues that to be a man a male must repudiate "women's values" such as interest in domestic life, nurturing, and collaborating. Such reasoning depends on Stoltenberg's misguided belief that there are "women's values." Moreover, there is no reason to believe that interest in domestic life or collaborative are "feminine" values.

Indeed, in places, Stoltenberg's paradigm turns into a diatribe against all men instead of the excesses of some. Unfortunately, an attack on all men *is* Stoltenberg's goal, and he acknowledges in the final essay of his book that the articulation of the radical feminism that he espouses "helped provide me with a form in which to express my anger at other men—an anger that in men can run very deep, as many of us know" (189). In essense, he uses his book, as too many men have used their fists, to attack those who are different from him. Nevertheless, some of his observations about father and son relationships hold true in examining the damaging relationships Toby has with Dwight and Roy. And because Stoltenberg's predictions that Toby will abandon his mother to avoid the wrath of a father proves false, *Refusing To Be A Man* further testifies to the strength of Toby's relationship with his mother.

III. SOUNDING LIKE A MAN

In the next section of this chapter, I want to look closely at the narrative voice in a single scene from *This Boy's Life*. Looking closely at the voice will allow me not only to articulate what I admire about Wolff's achievement as a writer but also to discuss, in a different way, the emotions and forces that affected Toby's childhood. To discuss the narrative voice, I want to use again the method of analyzing prose that Richard Lanham developed in *Analyzing Prose*. As I explained in the preceding chapter, I will, as Lanham does, spread the words of sentences across a page, showing how clauses are related to each other and what the natural rhythm of a passage looks like. In the left margin, I note the number of words in each sentence.

In this scene, Toby recalls a night when his mother went out on a date with a man she met earlier that afternoon at the Seattle SeaFair. While Rosemary is out, Toby is alone and worries about his mother.

5 I slept badly that night

13 I always did when my mother went out,
which wasn't often these days.

4 She came back late.

15 I listened to her walk up the stairs
and down the hall to our room.

5 The door opened and closed.

17 She stood just inside for a moment,
then crossed the room and sat down on her bed.

4 She was crying softly.

3 "Mom?" I said.

12 When she didn't answer
    I got up and went over to her.

3 "What's wrong, Mom?"

11 She looked at me,
    tried to say something,
    shook her head.

10 I sat beside her and put my arms around her.

10 She was gasping
    as if someone had held her underwater.

7 I rocked her and murmured to her.

27 I was practiced at this and happy doing it,
    not because she was unhappy
    but because she needed me,
  and to be needed made me feel capable.

4 Soothing her soothed me. (55)

The sentence structure here is strikingly different from what Angelou uses in *I Know Why the Caged Bird Sings*. Virtually all of Wolff's sentences are simple subject-verb sentences, the kind of sentences that Strunk and White would label "active sentences." Each of the first seven sentences in the passage begins with the subject and is immediately (or almost immediately) followed by its verb. (I slept . . . , I always did . . . , She came back . . . , I listened . . . , The door opened . . . , She stood . . . , She was crying . . .) Sentences 8 through 10 don't follow this pattern, but then the next 6 sentences return to the subject verb pattern of the first seven sentences. This is what Lanham loosely labels as "masculine prose." It is active and lean; there are few adjectives and even fewer descriptions.

The sentences' simplicity precludes them from explicating causal relationships. We are told Toby didn't sleep well on the nights his mother was out, but it is left to us to decide if this is cause and effect. We are told that the door opened and closed, but it is up to us to deduce who opened and shut it. Richard Lanham has argued that such style reveals a kind of nihilism, a world view where the speaker does not understand why things happen. Lanham dubs this Hemingway prose, because to him it sounds much like the prose Ernest Hemingway uses to describe the blasted world after the first world war. But certainly, too, this voice could be right for a child who cannot understand the whys of his world. Why is his mother crying? Why is their life so difficult? Why did his father leave him? These are "whys" Toby cannot answer, and the sentences Wolff uses to describe it reflect this reality here and in many places throughout *This Boy's Life*.

The length of sentences is also fundamentally different from that of many authors, particularly Maya Angelou. Wolff's sentences here are extremely short. In 16 sentences there are 131 words—an average of 8 words per sentence. This prose reports action but does not describe it. There are virtually no adjectives, noun phrases, adverbs. It is brief and matter of fact, the tight lipped prose of hard boiled detective stories, of Hemingway and Raymond Carver. And yet, the scene itself is very emotional. Toby is hugging his mother after she has been hurt. He hugs her, comforts her, rocks her. The only long sentence is the one in which he explains why he liked to hug his mother:

> I was practiced at this and happy doing it,
> not because she was unhappy
> but because she needed me,
> and to be needed made me feel capable.

The explanation is moving: she needed him and to be needed made him feel "capable." The final sentence is the most poignant. "Soothing her soothed me." The chiasmas gives a rhythmic, somnolent quality to the equally balanced halves of the sentence. It is almost like a cradle rocking back and forth. Soothing her (pause) soothed me.

Thus, while the prose takes on all the trappings of what Lanham has labeled "masculine prose" (lean, direct, factual), it reveals a very tender moment. In this sense the merging of style and content reveals the opposing desires—to be tender and tough-- that whipsaw Tobias Wolff as he grows up. He wants his mother's love but he also wants to project toughness to impress the men who surround him.

The paragraphs that follow this passage remind us, however, that Toby is also just a boy and *This Boy's Life* is about a boy's childhood. After he has comforted his mother, Toby helps her into her bed and the two of them fall asleep holding hands. In the morning, they don't discuss the night before. But in the end, Toby can't help but ask questions. The man who took Rosemary to dinner had promised to buy Toby a bike, and Toby wants to know about that bike. (I will again present this section in Lanhamesque form. But it is significant to note that this passage in Lanham form looks only slightly different from how it looks in the published text.)

(9) In the morning we were shy with each other.

(9) I somehow managed not to ask her my questions.

(15) That night, I continued to master myself,
but my self-mastery seemed like an act.

(10) I knew I was too weak to keep it up.

(4) My mother was reading.

(3) "Mom?" I said.

(3) She looked up.

(4) "What about the Raleigh?"

(8) She went back to her book without answering.

(5) I did not ask again. (56)

He is a boy who loves his mother deeply, but he also wants the possession prized by most boys his age: a bike. This tension between what child psychologist Karl Rodgers would refer to as the real self and the ideal self is something Toby is constantly aware of. Much of his childhood seems to be the record of conflict between the boy he is and the idealized young man that he feels he should be, between being strong and independent or being "too weak to keep it up."

This conflict, this tension between being the boy he is and being the mythical "all-American boy," permeates all of *This Boy's Life*. Throughout the text we are constantly aware that Toby wants to be somebody else, wants to be the idealized all-American boy, the elegant stranger who goes to prep school and is a star swimmer and "A" student. Ultimately, at the end of Toby's childhood, he achieves some of this dream, in large part through the unconditional love of his mother. Yet long before he leaves for prep school, Toby turns to writing to develop a sanctuary where he can pretend to be the boy that he wants to be, the multi-talented athletic boy whose father loves him. It is this ability to write, to articulate his vision of the boy he wants to be and the world he wants to live in that, ironically, helps him escape from the boy he is.

When he is living in Utah, Toby writes long letters to an Arizona pen pal named Alice. He describes to her, *as fact*, the fantasy life he wants to be living. He tells her that he lives on his father's ranch, rides a palomino horse, has adventures with mountain lions and rattlesnakes, raises german shepherds, and plays for several athletic teams. His yearning to be competent, independent, and 100% male is everywhere apparent. He does not live in a split level house that his mother has decorated but rather on a ranch in the desert with only his *father*. He doesn't ride a bike; he rides a horse. He doesn't play with cats or other little boys; he has adventures with dangerous animals and poisonous snakes. He doesn't raise guppies or poodles; he raises german shepherds.

A few years later, when he lives in Seattle, Toby stops writing to Alice and takes up writing to Annette Funicello of the Mickey Mouse Club. His letters tell the same "story" about his skills and courage but the specifics have changed. Now, he lives with his father, "Cap'n Wolff," who owns a fleet of fishing boats. As first mate, Toby is "a pretty fair hand at reeling in the big ones" and he takes the time to give Annette some detailed descriptions of his contests with the friskier fellows" (44). Again, through writing, Toby creates a world where he lives with his father on another frontier. He is competent and successful in the decidedly masculine world of seamen.

Toby next tries to create a better world for himself through writing the earlier mentioned letter to his uncle. Toby tries to convince his uncle and aunt to let him and his mother move in with them. He exaggerates their plight, plasters an envelope with stamps, and mails it off. In his concerned response, Toby's uncle offers to adopt Toby and let him live with their family in Paris, but Toby rejects the offer, for he feels he cannot leave his mother. His decision, as I've discussed above, is connected quite directly with the act of writing. In explaining his decision, Toby remembers how his mother taught him to write and sees their bond as one forged through writing:

> I was my mother's son. I could not be anyone else's. When I was younger and having trouble learning to write, she sat me down at the kitchen table and covered my hand with hers and moved it through the alphabet for several nights running, and then through words and sentences until the motions assumed their own life, partly hers and partly mine. I could not, cannot, put pen to paper without having her with me. (142)

Not many months after writing his uncle, Toby dramatically changes his life through his writing—by forging an application to an elite boarding school. After talking to his brother, Toby decides to try to follow in his footsteps and go to prep school. But when Toby receives applications from half a dozen of these schools, he realizes that he can't be admitted because he doesn't have the experiences, credentials, and qualities that they are looking for. He is not the all-American boy they want. Initially, he is stymied:

> I was stumped. Whenever I looked at the forms I felt despair. Their whiteness seemed hostile and vast, Saharan. I had nothing to get me across. During the day, I composed high-flown circumlocutions, but at night, when it came to writing them down, I balked at their silliness. The forms stayed clean. When my mother pressed me to send them off, I transferred them to my locker at school and told her everything was taken care of. I did not trouble my teachers for praise they could not give me, or bother to have my collection of C's sent out. I was giving up—*being realistic*, as people liked to say, meaning the same thing. (209)

In time, Toby changes his mind and decides to write an application that describes the boy he could be, should be, would be if he lived in different circumstances. He gets his old friend Arthur to pilfer school stationary, blank transcript forms, and a stack of official envelopes. In short order, he is able to cross the Saharan whiteness of the applications. Using his imagination, his writing skill, and his belief in his ultimate worth as a human being (if not in his actual achievements as a boy in a rotten situation), Toby writes into being the boy he wants to be:

> Now the words came as easily as if someone were breathing them into my ear. I felt full of things that had to be said, full of stifled truth. That was what I thought I was writing—the truth. It was truth known only to me, but I believed in it more than I believed in the facts arrayed against it. I believed that in some sense not factually verifiable I was a straight-A student. In the same way, I believed that I was an Eagle Scout, and a powerful swimmer, and a boy of integrity. These were the ideas about myself that I had held on to for dear life. Now I gave them voice. (213)

To Toby, what he writes *is* truth, the inner truth about who he is. All he is doing is giving this "truth" a voice. The passage above continues, and shows just how truthful Toby believes his writing to be:

> I made no claims that seemed false to me. I did not say that I was a star quarterback or even a varsity football player, because even though I went out for football every year I never quickened to the lumpen spirit of the sport. The same was true of basketball. I couldn't feature myself sinking a last-second clincher from the key, as Elgin Baylor did for Seattle that year in the NCAA playoffs against San Francisco. Ditto school politics; the unending compulsion to test one's own popularity was baffling to me.
>
> These were not ideas I had of myself, and I did not propose to urge them on anyone else. I declined to say I was a football star, but I did invent a swimming team for Concrete High. The coach wrote a fine letter for me, and so did my teachers and the principal. They didn't gush. They wrote plainly about a gifted, upright boy who had already in his own quiet way exhausted the resources of his school and community. They had done what they could for him. Now they hoped that others would carry on the good work.
>
> I wrote without heat or hyperbole, in the words my teachers would have used if they had known me as I knew myself. These were their letters. And on the boy who lived in their letters, the

> splendid phantom who carried all my hopes, it seemed to me I saw, at last, my own face. (213-214)

In sum, Toby creates the boy he wants to be, could be in different circumstances. Of course, it is the all-American boy—one who plays sports, gets good grades, is upright and honest, terse and modest.

By writing these letters, Toby fundamentally changes his own life. In short order, he is admitted to The Hill School and takes on all the trappings of the "splendid phantom" he sees in the mirror of the haberdashery shop of the scene that began this chapter. Hill School is not the magic answer to Toby's problems; in fact, within the year, Toby get's kicked out of the school for drinking. Nevertheless, the move away from Dwight and Chinook puts Toby on to the right track that ultimately enables him to become a successful father, husband, and writer. How it is exactly that Toby survived Dwight and Roy's abuse, his own father's rejection, and Concrete High School is not wholly knowable. What is certain is that his mother's unconditional love and his own ability to write—to use language to create a forgiving world and ask for what he needed—helped him survive his childhood and go on to live and love well.

IV
Memoirs of a Girlhood among Ghosts: *The Woman Warrior*

> "Now, of course, I expected *The Woman Warrior* to be read from the women's lib angle and the Third World angle, the *Roots* angle; but it is up to the author to transcend trendy categories."
>
> —Maxine Hong Kingston

Maxine Hong Kingston's *The Woman Warrior* has received far more attention from literary scholars than the other autobiographies considered in this study. By 1996, the Modern Languages Association listed almost 100 scholarly articles that examine *The Woman Warrior*. By contrast, MLA listed fewer than a dozen articles that discuss *I Know Why the Caged Bird Sings*, fewer than a half dozen articles that consider *Brothers and Keepers*, and not a single article that explores *This Boy's Life*.

Kingston's unique narrative structure attracted some critics to write about *The Woman Warrior*. Yet, for the most part, literary scholars have chosen to write about Kingston's work in order to relate it to contemporary feminist critical theory and the on-going debate about a woman's place in a patriarchal society such as the United States. For example, Sarah Gilead examines *The Woman Warrior* and concludes that Kingston's work

> dramatizes a central problem in women's quest for selfhood in the patriarchy—conflicting desires to escape the burden of traditional limits of self-concept and ways of living, yet to retain links to traditional culture and its capacity to lend historical and social significance to the self. (44)

Echoing Gilead, Linda Hunt interprets *The Woman Warrior* as a commentary on the struggle a woman experiences as she tries to establish a place in a patriarchal society:

> Maxine Hong Kingston's autobiographical *The Woman Warrior* suggests that we need to pay attention to the contradictions male dominance creates for women who are at one and the same time subordinated by a culture, and yet, embroiled in its interstices; such women may be painfully at odds with themselves. (5)

And Elizabeth Ordonez examines *The Woman Warrior*'s structuring as part of a "textual coding" that "becomes both the means and embodiment of modifying and reshaping female history, myths, and ultimately personal and collective identity" (19). The evolution of this new discourse may become "an alternate form of matrilineal discourse" that will provide women with the "potential to reshape our future as we reread our past" (27).

Gilead, Hunt, and Ordonez have each insightfully discussed what *The Woman Warrior* reveals about a woman's struggle to find a place in a male dominated society. Yet none of them—indeed no critic—has considered how Kingston's work compares with other stories about childhoods and what Kingston's work says about the life of children. All three authors—and dozens of others—fail to recognize that *The Woman Warrior* is subtitled *Memoirs of a Girlhood Among Ghosts*.

Unfortunately, this is all too often the case when adult critics look at the autobiographies of children. Adult critics are quick to recognize the relevance of a work as commentary on the issues of their own (adult) lives and their own adult intellectual interest in literary theory. They too rarely consider the relevance of works as commentary about the lives of children and growing up. By writing this, I am not dismissing the importance of the work of critics who examine the book as it relates to feminist theory and a woman's role in the patriarchy. Nor, in my own examination of Kingston's work, will I ignore the central importance of gender; the biological fact that Maxine Hong was a girl and not a boy profoundly affected her childhood. Nevertheless, I want to do what literary critics have not done: consider *The Woman Warrior: Memoirs of a Girlhood Among Ghosts* as part of a congeries of books that offer perspectives on childhood. I want to do this because Kingston's work, like *This Boy's Life*, *Hunger of*

Memory, *I Know Why the Caged Bird Sings*, and *Brothers and Keepers*, offers insights on many of the central themes and conflicts that we have already seen in childhood autobiographies.

I. "YOU MUST NOT TELL ANYONE"

Maxine Hong Kingston begins her memoirs about her childhood by recalling a story about her menarche. When Maxine began to menstruate, her mother came to her and told her that she needed to tell Maxine a story—but it was a story Maxine could never repeat:

> "You must not tell anyone," my mother said, "what I am about to tell you" (1).

These are the opening words of *The Woman Warrior*. Their primacy of place stand as evidence, I think, of Kingston's deeply felt belief that her family and the two cultures she lived in (Chinese and American) were constantly trying to keep her quiet. The tale her mother tells offers an effective place to begin to describe the obstacles that faced Maxine Hong Kingston during her childhood.

The tale Maxine's mother tells her daughter is about an unmarried aunt who lived in rural China and got pregnant. The consequences to the aunt and the unborn child were severe. Just before the child was due, the villagers disguised themselves in white masks and stormed the aunt's home:

> "The villagers broke in the front and the back doors at the same time, even though we had not locked the doors against them. Their knives dripped with the blood of our animals. They smeared blood on the doors and walls. One woman swung a chicken, whose throat she had slit, splattering blood in red arcs about her. We stood together in the middle of our house, in the family hall with the pictures and tables of the ancestors around us, and looked straight ahead.
>
> ". . . They ripped up her clothes and shoes and broke her combs, grinding them underfoot. They tore her work from the loom. They scattered the cooking fire and rolled the new weaving in it. We could hear them in the kitchen breaking our bowls and banging the

> pots. They overturned the great waist-high earthenware jugs; duck eggs, pickled fruits, vegetables burst out and mixed in acrid torrents. The old woman from the next field swept a broom through the air and loosed the spirits-of-the-broom over our heads. 'Pig.' 'Ghost.' 'Pig,' they sobbed and scolded while they ruined our house. (4-5)

The aunt gave birth to her child that night and then drowned herself and the child in the family well. For ever after, the family and the villagers never mentioned the aunt's name; for transgressing the community mores, she was expunged from the community memory and denied any existence whatsoever.

After Maxine's mother tells the story, she again demands that Maxine never reveal that she knows the history of her aunt: "Don't let your father know that I told you. He denies her" (5). Her mother's demand that the tragedy remain hidden testifies to the patriarchal nature of Chinese culture and, of course, the unquestioned authority of Maxine's father.

Yet the opening pages of *The Woman Warrior* do not end here. Maxine Hong Kingston cannot forget the story. Reflecting on her aunt's story many years after she heard it, Kingston writes her own belief that in all probability her aunt had not chosen to have intercourse, but rather had been raped and then humiliated for getting pregnant:

> My aunt could not have been the lone romantic who gave up everything for sex. Women in the Old China did not choose. Some man had commanded her to lie with him and be his secret evil. I wonder whether he masked himself when he joined the raid on her family. (6)

Thus the opening pages of *The Woman Warrior* not only document the ability of men to silence women in Kingston's family but also testifies to the longer history of Chinese women being abused and then silenced by men. It is this double bind—of being subservient and silenced—created by family and culture that makes Maxine's childhood so difficult, her resilience so inspiring.

Beginning the memoirs of her girlhood with the story of her aunt, Maxine Hong Kingston provides a strong foundation on which to add further memories that document the attempts to control and silence her throughout her girlhood. Indeed, *The Woman Warrior* is filled with insults and slights that Maxine experienced because she, like Maya Angelou, lived in a family and in a culture that privileged boys.

Early in *The Woman Warrior* Kingston remembers that on most Saturdays her great uncle came to her family's home to pick up the children on his way to do the weekly shopping. Maxine's brothers quickly grabbed their coats and ran to the door, but when Maxine and her sister did the same, the great uncle turned around and roared, "No girls!" The males went off together, while the females were left at home to clean the house and prepare dinner. Her brothers returned from these expeditions with candy and new toys.

Later in *The Woman Warrior*, Kingston recalls when she and her sisters had dinner with three other girls and their great grandfather insulted all of them:

> The old man opened his eyes wide at us and turned in a circle, surrounded [by girls]. His neck tendons stretched out. "Maggots!" he shouted. "Maggots! Where are my grandsons? I want grandsons! Give me grandsons! Maggots!" He pointed at each one of us, "Maggot! Maggot! Maggot! Maggot! Maggot! Maggot!" Then he dived into his food, eating faster and getting seconds. "Eat, maggots," he said.
>
> "He does that at every meal," the girls told us in English.
>
> "Yeah," we said, "Our old man hates us too. What assholes." (191)

And she remembers that when she and her sisters were born, her family held no public celebration. But when her brothers were born, the family followed Chinese tradition and held a month-long party. Pictures of new born male children were sent to relatives in China; no pictures of new born female children were sent anywhere.

The privileging of her brothers hurt Maxine, but so too did an endless series of misogynist aphorisms that Maxine's family members and neighbors commonly repeat. Throughout her girlhood and throughout *The Woman Warrior*, Kingston remembers the many times that her neighbors and her family would say things such as "There is no profit in raising girls." "When you raise girls, you are raising children for strangers." "Better to raise geese than girls." "Feeding girls is like feeding cowbirds, there's no benefit in it." "When fishing for treasures in the flood, be careful not to pull in girls." These sayings scalded Maxine, driving a wedge between her and her family:

> But I watched such words come out of my own mother's and father's mouths; I looked at their ink drawing of poor people snagging their neighbor's flotage with long flood hooks and pushing the girl babies on down the river. And I had to get out of hating range. (52)

The defining experiences of Maxine's childhood seem to involve the abuse and insults she suffered. In many ways, one of the *raisons d'etre* of *The Woman Warrior* is for Kingston to report, first hand, crimes against Chinese females. The insults are so hurtful that ultimately she comes to dream of becoming a modern day Chinese warrior. Instead of using a sword to behead the cruel and greedy land barons of ancient China, she will use a pen to slash the modern day misogynists and report their cruelties.

Indeed, Kingston advances this analogy at the close of the second chapter. She notes how before they began their attack, the ancient Chinese warriors often had the crimes of their enemies carved into their backs. Kingston asserts that, like these Chinese warriors, she too has words, the hateful cruel words of misogyny, carved into her back. By reporting, in words, the cruelties, she avenges the crime:

> The swordswoman and I are not so dissimilar. May my people understand the resemblance soon so that I can return to them. What we have in common are the words at our backs. The idioms for "revenge" are "report a crime" and "report to five families." The reporting is the vengeance—not the beheading, not the gutting, but the words. And I have so many words—"chink" words and "gook" words too—that they do not fit on my skin. (53)

Thus, *The Woman Warrior*, because it reports the crimes of family and community, is an act of revenge. With the final words of the passage above, the recognition that she has also been hurt by "chink" and "gook" words, Kingston draws attention to the racism that shaped her childhood and, of course, the childhoods of Maya Angelou, Richard Rodriguez, and John and Robby Wideman.

Throughout much of her childhood, Kingston recalls that she felt isolated, uncomfortable with her non-Chinese peers at school and uncertain about appropriate behavior in the mostly Anglo schools of Stockton, California. Kingston recalls that throughout her entire first year in school, she never spoke. Less familiar with English than the other students and well schooled by her community to abide by their cultural more of girls being silent, Maxine spoke not one word that first year.

Misinterpreting her silence as intellectual dullness, Maxine's teacher required her to repeat kindergarten. It was only in her second year of kindergarten that Maxine finally realized that she was supposed to speak in school. This made her miserable:

> It was when I found out I had to talk that school became a misery, that the silence became a misery. I did not speak and felt bad each time that I did not speak" (166).

Her silence also makes her exceedingly vulnerable. Japanese-American children hit her and stuck gum in her ears. Her teacher continued to ignore her.

By the time she reaches first grade, Maxine ventures to read aloud, in whispers and squeaks. Her teacher's response is to demand that she speak louder, and that command scares Maxine's voice away. Maxine is not alone in her timidity: "The other Chinese girls did not talk either, so I knew the silence had to do with being a Chinese girl." Her teacher puts her in the "low corner under the stairs, where the noisy boys usually sat" (166). When the class puts on a play, Maxine's teacher leaves the Chinese girls in the classroom, rather than include them in a choral reading or group recitation.

One day, Maxine must recite a lesson to the entire class. Kingston's description of the experience points out just how difficult speaking aloud was for her:

> When it was my turn, the same voice came out, a crippled animal running on broken legs. You could hear splinters in my voice, bones rubbing jagged against one another. I was loud, though. I was glad I didn't whisper. There was one little girl who whispered. (169)

Yet while Maxine ultimately learns to speak in public, she feels that she is never on equal footing with the other children in her class and, perhaps worst of all, she feels she can never earn the respect of her own family. She continues to hear the misogynist sayings, she continues to see her brothers given special treatment, and she continues to be expected to carry out all the domestic chores of cooking, cleaning, and shopping while her brothers are coddled and encouraged to get the best possible education. When she earns straight A's in school, neighbors tell her that the good grades are valuable only because they will help her to better serve her future husband.

Yet, ultimately, Maxine finishes high school, gets a scholarship to Berkeley, and is able to develop a strong sense of self and a clear voice with which to write *The Woman Warrior*. Whereas most of the critical commentary on Kingston's work has focused on all the injustices and frustrations Maxine faced, Kingston's work also documents the people and forces—including her culture—that gave her the resilience she needed to survive her childhood. Kingston's mother, referred to throughout *The Woman Warrior* by her family name of Brave Orchid, plays the most central role in the development of Maxine's resilience and her empowerment, as we will see in the next section.

II. "I CUT YOUR TONGUE TO MAKE YOU TALK MORE, NOT LESS, YOU DUMMY!"

Even before she learns how to speak, Maxine listens to her mother as she tells Maxine infinite and varied stories about heroic Chinese women. Using the Chinese oral tradition of talk-story, Brave Orchid fills her daughter's mind with stories about powerful women and simultaneously tries, directly and subliminally, to discourage Maxine from becoming "just" a wife or a slave:

> When we Chinese girls listened to [our mother] talk-story, we learned that we failed if we grew up to be but wives or slaves. We could be heroines, swordswomen. (19)

Night after night, Maxine falls asleep while her mother tells her stories about heroines. Early in *The Woman Warrior*, Kingston acknowledges the power of her mother's stories:

> At last I saw that I too had been in the presence of great power, my mother talking-story. After I grew up, I heard the chant of Fa Mu

> Lan, the girl who took her father's place in battle. Instantly I remembered that as a child I had followed my mother about the house, the two of us singing about how Fa Mu Lan fought gloriously and returned alive from war to settle in the village. I had forgotten this chant that was once mine, given me by my mother, who may not have known its power to remind. She said I would grow up a wife and a slave but she taught me the song of the warrior woman, Fa Mu Lan. *I would have to grow up a warrior woman.* (19-20 emphasis mine)

From these stories, Maxine begins to shape her powerful future.

Early in *The Woman Warrior: Memoirs of a Girlhood Among Ghosts*, Kingston uses a literary device to show just how much her mother's stories affected her psyche. After recording, in the passage cited immediately above, how she and her mother would sing songs about woman warriors and Fa Mu Lan, Kingston suddenly changes her narrative line and describes how one day she was transported through a forest and over the tallest mountains into a new world above the clouds. During the next twenty-five pages of *The Woman Warrior*, Kingston describes how an old man and woman trained her to become a woman warrior just like Fa Mu Lan. First, they teach her how to remain silent for a full day. Next, she learns how to control her body completely. After six years, she can run alongside deer and jump twenty feet in the air. Then she begins her training as a swordswomen. After a decade's work, she is ferocious and unbeatable. She returns to her family and with the words describing their grievances carved into her back, she goes out and executes those who have wronged her family.

Some of my college students have been confused by the section that describes Maxine training to be a swordswomen. Kingston never lets on that the passage is sheer fantasy—that she did not spend twenty years practicing to be a swordswomen. Kingston's writing is so matter of fact that several of my students have been completely hoodwinked. "Did she really train like that?" several have asked. "I couldn't follow what was true and what was a dream," others have complained. Yet, as their more imaginative peers have pointed out, the sleight of hand and resulting initial confusion coincides with what Kingston has just asserted--that as a child she "couldn't tell where the stories left off and the dreams began." Moreover, as the more reflective students point out, the long digression documents that Maxine's childhood, her dreams and her self-identity, were dramatically affected by the stories her mother told her about the woman warrior. The stories provide Maxine with heroines and aspirations, a fantasy world that can inspire her despite all the misogyny and chauvinism that surround her. The stories are not only the armor that protects her, but they also provide the strength that empowers her.

Through talk-story, Maxine benefits from her mother's great skill and potent imagination; the stories not only tell of the powers of women warriors, they also document the powers that her mother has. Joanne Frye, in "*The Woman Warrior*: Claiming Narrative Power, Recreating Female Selfhood," makes this point quite well:

> The tale [of Fa Mu Lan] becomes [Maxine's] protection against her hostile surroundings, but it is not a fantastic escape from a harsh reality, as might be implied in the contrast between "slaves" and "swordswomen" or in the allusion to women's once dangerous powers. Rather the tale is itself rooted in her harsh daily reality and assumes for itself and for her a reality of its own . . . This reality then—the power of her mother as a real woman and as a storyteller—is the source of the knowledge present in the subjunctive become indicative, the impetus for the personal legend, and *the basis for creating a selfhood rooted in reality, strengthened through fantasy, and evolved through the narrative process.* (296, emphasis mine)

Her mother's stories invest Maxine with dreams and goals, while her mother's story-telling gives her an understanding of how words and the narrative process can empower her. In this sense, Brave Orchid's story telling is reminiscent not only of Mrs. Flowers' encouraging Maya to speak, but also Tobias Wolff's mother teaching him to write. This is fundamentally important. To become independent and successful, children must have adults who believe in their abilities and who, through example and encouragement, give them confidence and support. As we have seen and will see in each chapter, adults play a critical role in building resilience in children.

Although Maxine's mother sings about the lives of famous Chinese heroines, her own life is at least as inspiring as the lives of the women she sings about. We see this in "Shaman," the long, third chapter of *The Woman Warrior*. "Shaman" is almost entirely about the life of Maxine's mother, her heroism and courage in the face of innumerable hardships. The chapter proves beyond the shadow of a doubt that Brave Orchid was well named. I read this chapter about Brave Orchid to be the epicenter of *The Woman Warrior*. At the simple, literal level, the chapter *is* at the center of the book; it is the third of five chapters and includes the middle pages of the work. At a subtler, more substantive level, "Shaman" is at the epicenter of *The Woman Warrior* because Brave Orchid is the most important figure in Maxine's childhood. By example and by talk-story, Brave Orchid inspires her daughter and serves as the catalyst for much of Maxine's growth and independence. Indeed, the entire book can be read as Maxine's effort to understand and thank her mother.

Brave Orchid has lived an extraordinary life. Alterntively, she has been courageous, cunning, relentless, shrewd, brutal, maternal, and pragmatic. In "Shaman," Kingston recounts several of the stories her mother told about her own life; each one shows the profound strength of Brave Orchid. The first story is about her mother's experience as a medical student. When Brave Orchid was 30, her husband left her to go to the United States where he planned to make his fortune and then send for her. Although Brave Orchid's husband regularly mailed her money, he never sent for her. Two years pass and despite Brave Orchid's frantic efforts, both her children die. Brave Orchid continues to wait for word from her husband. Finally, she gives up on him and decides, at age 35, to sail to the Medical School in the capital city of her province and begin studying to become a doctor.

At medical school, Brave Orchid, although she had been out of school for close to 20 years, becomes the best student. She studies relentlessly and earns the highest grades. When the other students become convinced that there are ghosts in their dormitory, Brave Orchid volunteers to investigate. She has faced terrors far worse than unseen ghosts—she has buried her two children and been abandoned by her husband—so she thinks little of offering to spend the night in the storage room where the younger students think the ghosts reside. During the night, she, in fact, feels a ghost come sit on her chest, but she shows no fear. She imagines that this ghost is the murderer of her babies and lashes out:

> "I do not give in," she said. "There is no pain you can inflict that I cannot endure. You're wrong if you think I'm afraid of you. You're no mystery to me. I've heard of you Sitting Ghosts before. Yes, people have lived to tell about you. You kill babies, you cowards. You have no power over a strong woman. You are no more dangerous than a nesting cat. My dog sits on my feet more heavily than you can. You think this is suffering? I can make my ears ring louder by taking aspirin. Are these all the tricks you have, Ghost? Sitting and ringing? That is nothing. A Broom Ghost can do better. (70)

Her fellow students hear her talking to the ghost and in the morning proclaim her a hero. For the remainder of her two years of studies, she is not only the star student but also the class leader.

For the next five years, Brave Orchid does what few Chinese women did: she establishes her own medical practice. Then, when the Japanese threaten to overrun much of China, Brave Orchid sails to the United States and tracks down her husband. At forty-three, she begins a second family with him. In the ensuing years, she gives birth to six children. Unable to start a medical practice in the United States, she and her husband start a laundry and work the many hours under the difficult conditions that most small businesses require.

When she is not working in the laundry, she is running the household using the meager profits of the business as best she can. She is brutally frugal. She cooks whatever they can afford, including skunk, turtle, and squid. And the children must eat what she prepares or see it served again and again until it is gone. Maxine remembers

> We'd have to face four- and five-day-old leftovers until we ate it all. The squid eye would keep appearing at breakfast and dinner until eaten. Sometimes brown masses sat on every dish. I have seen revulsion on the faces of visitors who've caught us at meals. (92)

For Maxine, the meals testified to her mother's pragmatism and strength just as her career as a doctor testified to her intelligence and independence.

In a typically inspirational interview, Maya Angelou declared that "everyone lives in relation to their heroes and she-roes" (Elliot 112). Angelou's point is that human beings live and achieve according to the people they admire and try to emulate. In the second chapter, we witnessed the impact of two "she-roes:" Bertha Flowers and Maya's grandmother. In the third chapter, we saw the impact Rosemary Wolff had on Tobias. In this chapter, Brave Orchid is the she-roe, and as much as anyone or anything, she builds Maxine's resilience.

Two scenes described late in *The Woman Warrior* exemplify the impact that Brave Orchid had on her daughter and document how she helps Maxine break free from the patriarchal society and limited expectations that surrounded her. As Maxine enters adolescence, she is able and willing to speak aloud in class and to participate in the athletic games of the other children. Nevertheless, she is acutely aware of another classmate, a Chinese girl, who steadfastly plays the role of the silent subservient Chinese girl that Maxine has learned to reject. Always dressed in extremely feminine clothes and always sporting a Chinese doll hair cut, this girl never speaks. When the children play games, she is always the last chosen and her attempts at even the simplest sport are pathetic.

One day after school, Maxine and this silent little girl find themselves alone in the girls bathroom. Maxine decides that now is the time to make this little girl speak:

> "You're going to talk," I said, my voice steady and normal, as it is when talking to the familiar, the weak, and the small. "I am going to make you talk, you sissy-girl." She stopped backing away and stood fixed.
>
> I looked into her face so I could hate it close up . . .
>
> I reached up and took the fatty part of her cheek, not dough, but meat, between my thumb and finger. This close, and I saw no pores. "Talk," I said. "Are you going to talk?" Her skin was fleshy, like squid out of which the glassy blades of bones had been pulled. (175-176)

For the next quarter hour, Maxine tries all ways imaginable to get the little girl to speak. Pinching her, yelling into her ears, pulling her pigtails, Maxine only gets silence. Maxine then gets rougher—pulling hair out of the little girl's temples, shaking her, even threatening to kill her. Nothing works. At wits end, Maxine finally tries to reason with her and tells her this is for her own good:

> You don't see I'm trying to help you out, do you? Do you want to be like this, dumb (do you know what dumb means?), your whole life? Don't you ever want to be a cheerleader? Or a pompon girl? What are you going to do for a living? Yeah, you're going to have to work because you can't be a housewife. Somebody has to marry you before you can be a housewife. And you, you are a plant. Do you know that? That's all you are if you don't talk. If you don't talk, you can't have a personality. You'll have no personality and no hair. You've got to let people know you have a personality and a brain. You think somebody is going to take care of you all your stupid life? (180)

Maxine cannot get the girl to speak. Finally, the girl's older sister finds her charge and leads her little sister, still silent, away from Maxine.

In her effort to get her classmate to speak, Maxine reveals the impact of her mother's example and the stories about women warriors and house slaves. The silent girl embodies the role that Maxine has learned to reject. Maxine feels she must get the girl to speak and thereby reject the role of houseslave. It's interesting, of course, to note that language—the use of language—is the central issue of this central scene, just as using language is critical to central scenes already discussed in *I Know Why The Caged Bird Sings* and *This Boy's Life*, and will be central to the central chapters of *Hunger of Memory* and *Brothers and Keepers.* In all these stories, silence insures that a child will conform to a culturally determined identity; language confers the power to break from this position of powerlessness.

In her conflict with the silent Chinese girl, Maxine fails. The girl never does speak. And Maxine is horrified at her brutality. Consequently, she regresses beyond the behavior of the silent girl and the point of Maya Angelou after her rape. Maxine stops speaking and becomes a recluse:

> The world is sometimes just, and I spent the next eighteen months sick in bed with a mysterious illness. There was no pain and no symptoms, though the middle line in my left palm broke in two. Instead of starting junior high school, I lived like the Victorian recluses I read about. I had a rented hospital bed in the living room, where I watched soap operas on t.v. , and my family cranked me up

> and down. I saw no one but my family, who took good care of me. I could have no visitors, no other relatives, no villagers. (181-182)

Most appropriately, it is Maxine's mother who ends Maxine's paralysis. After a year of coddling her daughter, Brave Orchid announces one day "You're ready to get up today. It's time to get up and go to school." And as simple as that, Maxine immediately rises from her bed and goes to school.

Back in school, Maxine starts to talk again and in little time returns to earning straight A's. But she never believes that she has the total respect of her family and her mother. In her senior year of high school, Maxine explodes. Believing that her mother is trying to marry her off to a rich but semi-retarded boy who hangs around the laundry and carries with him a box of pornography, Maxine finally blows up:

> I want you to tell that hunk, that gorilla-ape, to go away and never bother us again. I know what you're up to. You're thinking he's rich, and we're poor. You think we're odd and not pretty and we're not bright. You think you can give us away to freaks. You better not do that, Mother. I don't want to see him or his dirty boxes here tomorrow. If I see him here one more time, I'm going away. I'm going away anyway. I am. I may be ugly and clumsy, but one thing I'm not, I'm not retarded. There's nothing wrong with my brain. Do you know what the Teacher Ghosts say about me? They tell me I'm smart, and I can win scholarships. I can get into colleges. I've already applied. I'm smart. I can do all kinds of things. I know how to get A's, and they say I could be a scientist or a mathematician if I want. I can make a living and take care of myself . . . I'm so smart, if they say write ten pages, I can write fifteen. I can do ghost things even better than ghosts can. Not everybody thinks I'm nothing. I'm not going to be a slave or a wife. (201)

In a very real sense, this is the climax of *The Woman Warrior*: Maxine has become a true warrior. She has developed her sense of self-worth ("I'm smart. I can do all kinds of things."), and she has also mastered the ability of articulating her worth. She can speak, use her own words and her own thoughts to assert herself. She is independent, and, as she declares, will go away to college and then on to a new life.

Yet, this is *not* the final scene of *The Woman Warrior*. There is, in fact, a final chapter in which mother and daughter reunite, reach a reconciliation and a mutual appreciation of who each is and what they have each accomplished. This scene, which makes up the very final pages of *The Woman Warrior*, makes clear the role Brave Orchid played in shaping Maxine's identity. Before we look at this final scene, however, I want to pay a little more attention to the voice and the structuring that Kingston uses to describe her childhood among ghosts. Doing this will, I think, provide a useful way to understand that final scene and just who Maxine Hong Kingston is at the end of *The Woman Warrior*. To discuss Kingston's voice and structuring, I want to bring in Jade Snow Wong's childhood autobiography, *Fifth Chinese Daughter*, as a useful foil for this discussion.

III. "I" VERSUS "SHE," "WARRIOR" VERSUS "DAUGHTER"

In 1950, when she was writing *Fifth Chinese Daughter*, Jade Snow Wong had demonstrably different goals than Maxine Hong Kingston had twenty-five years later when she was writing *The Woman Warrior*. When Wong was writing *Fifth Chinese Daughter*, she realized that "nothing had been published [in the United States] from a female Chinese American perspective." Consequently, she wrote "with the purpose of creating better understanding of the Chinese culture on the part of Americans." With this goal in mind, Wong offered a respectful and positive depiction of Chinese culture.

Like Kingston, Wong endured a childhood in which her parents privileged their sons and demanded that their daughters tend to the housework. Yet Wong glosses over these inequities and, as we will see, rationalizes them as a minor problem in an extraordinarily rich culture. Indeed, Wong presents the mirror image of Chinese culture that Kingston produces; whereas Kingston details and challenges all that was unfair, misogynist, and debilitating about Chinese culture, Wong focuses on the positive elements of her Chinese heritage.

In a 1989 preface to a re-issuing of *Fifth Chinese Daughter*, Wong notes with pride that while she was raising her children she often gave her career as an artist a lower priority so that she could live in accordance with the traditional role of Chinese mothers:

> [From 1956 to 1968] I developed my ceramic arts and mothered two sons and two daughters. Husband and children knew that they held priority over my career. I have spent more time at my kitchen stove than at my kilns. It has been said that food, family, and endurance (in that order) characterize Chinese consciousness. Each of my children did homework in the kitchen while I coached and cooked, and each is now able to create delicious innovations at the wok. (viii)

Wong also describes with great pride how she and her husband have brought up their children so that they appreciate Chinese culture and embody what she believes are the fundamental values of the Chinese people:

> My husband and I chose our home within walking distance of Chinatown so that each child could attend six years of the same Christian Chinese evening school I had. And though they then protested the burden of their studies, which their friends escaped, as adults they are glad to understand the tongue their friends do not. They know well that, in behavior, we emphasize personal modesty, self-reliance, dependability, courtesy, and modulated voices. In values, we esteem love of books and learning, reverence for the natural world, service to fellow man, moderation, living within one's means. Are these values different from those of non-Chinese? Our basic and greatest value is family cohesiveness. From time immemorial, in every culture, for every economic station, the family is the enduring motivation of human activity. Ours is grateful for our Chinese past. (x)

Wong ends the 1989 preface by celebrating her bicultural heritage and the opportunities it has brought her. She concludes, "With the plus of our rich cultural heritage, to be an Asian in America is our distinction" (xi).

Maxine Hong Kingston, of course, would never refer to herself as "an Asian in America." Although both women were born to first generation Chinese American parents, Wong refers to herself as an "Asian in America" while Kingston has repeatedly taken offence at such references. When *The Woman Warrior* was published and many reviewers referred to her as "Chinese," Kingston angrily responded to these references in an article entitled "Cultural Mis-readings by American Reviewers." Two representative quotations of Kingston's article are:

> Another bothersome characteristic of the reviews is the ignorance of the fact that I am an American. I am an American writer, who, like other American writers, wants to write the great American novel. *The Woman Warrior* is an American book. Yet many reviewers do not see the American-ness of it, nor the fact of my own American-ness. (57-58)
>
> . . . . .
>
> *The Saturday News and Leader* of Springfield Missouri: "Maxine Ting Hong Kingston is a Chinese woman, even though the place of her birth was Stockton, California." This does not make sense. *Because* I was born in Stockton, California, I *am* an American woman. I am also a Chinese American woman, but I am not a Chinese woman, never having travelled east of Hawaii, unless she means an 'ethnic Chinese woman," in which case she should say so. (58)

Kingston claims she wants her story to "bust through any stereotypes" and present her as an American and not as a Chinese woman.

While the comments of both authors outside of their original texts are worth considering, more important—and indeed more revealing—are the differences within the texts, especially in voice and structure. One of the most striking stylistic difference between the two works revolves around something as simple as self-reflexive pronouns, how each author refers to herself in the text. Kingston uses the first person "I" to represent Maxine. Wong uses the third person "she." *Fifth Chinese Daughter* opens

> Until she was five years old, Jade Snow's world was almost wholly Chinese, for her world was her family, the Wongs. Life was secure but formal, sober but quietly happy, and the few problems she had were entirely concerned with what was proper or improper in the behavior of a little Chinese girl. (2)

And *Fifth Chinese Daughter* ends

> As for Jade Snow, she knew that she still had before her a hard upward climb, but for the first time in her life, she felt contentment. She could stop searching for that niche that would be hers alone. She had found herself and struck her speed. And when she came home now, it was to see Mama and Daddy look up from their work, and smile at her, and say, "It is good to have you home again!" (246)

In the author's note to the original edition of *Fifth Chinese Daughter*, Wong explains her choice of using third person as a way of keeping with Chinese tradition of self-effacement and respect:

> Although a "first person singular" book, this story is written in the third person from Chinese habit. The submergence of the individual is literally practiced. In written Chinese, prose or poetry, the word "I" almost never appears, but is understood. In corresponding with an older person like my father, I would write in words half the size of the regular ideographs, "small daughter Jade Snow" when referring to myself; to one of contemporary age, I would put in small characters, "younger sister"—but never "I." Should my father, who owes me no respect, write to me, he would still refer to himself in the third person, "Father." *Even written in English, an "I" book by a Chinese would seem outrageously immodest to anyone raised in the spirit of Chinese propriety.* (xiii, emphasis mine)

Jade Snow Wong's references to her book as a "book by a Chinese" reiterates her sense of identity as a Chinese (and not Chinese American) person, as does her matter of fact observation that her father owes her no respect. Wong's use of third person gives *Fifth Chinese Daughter* a distant tone, a tone that establishes a sense of propriety not only between Jade Snow and her readers but also between Jade Snow and her parents. Unlike Kingston, Wong refuses to challenge or criticize her parents.

One emblematic example of this comes when Wong's father tells her that he will not finance her college education because he wants to reserve money for her younger brother's medical school expenses. All that Maxine Hong Kingston rails against in *The Woman Warrior* is apparent in the rationale used by Jade Snow's father, who says:

> "You are quite familiar by now with the fact that it is the sons who perpetuate our ancestral heritage by permanently bearing the Wong family name and transmitting it through their blood line, and therefore the sons must have priority over the daughters when parental provision for advantages must be limited by economic necessity. Generations of sons, bearing our Wong name, are those who make pilgrimages to ancestral burial grounds and preserve them forever. Our daughters leave home at marriage to give sons to their husbands' families to carry on the heritage for other names. (108-109)

Indeed, Kingston might argue that Father Wong's rationale is an intellectualization of one of the aphorisms that sent Maxine into paroxysms of anger: "There's no profit in raising girls."

Jade Snow Wong, however, does not throw a tantrum when her father delivers his opinion, but rather retreats to her bedroom and tries to understand the reasoning:

> Jade Snow retreated to her little bedroom, but now she felt imprisoned. She was trapped in a mesh of tradition woven thousands of miles away by ancestors who had no knowledge that someday one generation of their progeny might be raised in another culture. Acknowledging that she owed her very being and much of her thinking to those ancestors and their tradition, she could not believe that this background was meant to hinder her further development, either in America or in China. (110)

She does not condemn the society or the culture that systematically denies girls a college education. Indeed, she defends the originators of that culture by rationalizing their "error" as one caused because they never knew that someone like herself would "be raised in another culture." She does not question that perhaps there would be use for a college education for women in China, as Brave Orchid demonstrated.

Maxine Hong Kingston's language and reasoning are of course far different. Kingston uses "I" throughout her story. She recounts how, as a child, she was taken aback by the American use of "I:"

> Reading out loud was easier than speaking because we did not have to make up what to say, but I stopped often, and the teacher would

> think I'd gone quiet again. I could not understand "I." . . . "I" is a capital and "you" is lower-case. I stared at that middle line and waited so long for its black center to resolve into tight strokes and dots that I forgot to pronounce it. (166-67)

Yet, *The Woman Warrior* makes clear that Maxine ultimately comes to use "I" like a self-assured and aggressive American. When Kingston, in a scene similar to the one just described from *Fifth Chinese Daughter*, announces that despite the lack of support from her parents she will go to college, her words, as I've argued earlier, demonstrate that she is not afraid to say "I":

> *I*'m going away. *I*'m going away anyway. *I* am. Do you hear me? *I* may be ugly and clumsy, but one thing *I*'m not, *I*'m not retarded. There's nothing wrong with my brain. Do you know what the Teacher Ghosts say about me? They tell me *I*'m smart, and *I* can win scholarships. *I* can get into colleges. *I*'ve already applied. *I*'m smart. *I* can do all kinds of things. *I* know how to get A's, and they say *I* could be a scientist or a mathematician if *I* want. (201, emphasis mine)

Indeed, of the first 500 words of the outburst, 50 are "I."

How each author structures her autobiography is just as revealing as the authors' choice of pronouns. Jade Snow Wong employs a traditional chronological structuring for her autobiography. Wong begins with her first memory ("Until she was five years old, Jade Snow's world was almost wholly Chinese . . . ") and proceeds, month by month, to tell the story of her childhood. First A happened, then B happened, then C happened: going to public school, the birth of her brother, Chinese New Year. Wong's structuring, similar to what Angelou and Wolff use, implies a clear order to life and, more significant, a deep-seated sense of cause and effect. B not only happened after A, in most cases, B happened *because* A happened.

Maxine Hong Kingston rejects the traditional chronological structuring of a life-story. *The Woman Warrior* is anything *but* a chronological account of Kingston's childhood. Indeed, as I noted earlier, some of my college students have difficulty following Kingston's narrative—following her abrupt transitions and recognizing relationships between figures that appear in the work.

Feminist critics such as Sandra Gilbert and Susan Gubar could argue that what Kingston has done is quintessentially feminist: she has rejected the traditional, linear, phallic, autocratic structures that men have established for autobiographies and replaced it with a non-linear, non-phallocentric, non-autocratic structure that focuses on creativity and inclusion.

At the most simplistic level, Kingston structures *The Woman Warrior* around people—some mythic, some real, some quasi-mythic, some quasi-real: the mythic woman warrior Fa Mu Lan, Brave Orchid, the aunt who committed suicide, Moon Orchid. Yet to simplify Kingston's structuring this way—to argue that its structure is constructed around individual people—is to oversimplify her work.

In each chapter, Kingston weaves the past and the present together, pulls in real and mythic figures, blurs the line between story and history. Each chapter is, in many ways, a celebration of inclusion—inclusion of the mythic and the mundane, ghosts and heroines, relatives and ancestors. By including all these elements and steering clear of a simpler chronologic recounting of her childhood, Kingston enriches her life story. We understand the influences in her life—the cultural myths and family stories—that shape her identity and give strength and resilience. While we never quite understand the precise details of her life, we do understand the conflicting and extraordinary influences that shape her. This structuring provides us with a wide angle view of Maxine Hong Kingston, even if some of the lines are fuzzy.

As described in the introductory chapter, James Olney acknowledges that language (and autobiography) cannot provide a one-to-one correlation to experience. Yet he argues that language and autobiography can provide a general sense of self. Olney believes that autobiography functions much like metaphor and myth; it offers a hazy, but at its core, accurate view of what is. Kingston's autobiography, more so than any of the other autobiographies examined, avoids what deconstructionists see as the problem with language: the inability of words to reveal reality. Surely, woe comes to those who try to nail down exactly what happened in Maxine Hong Kingston's childhood. Yet, as Olney argues, satisfaction does come to those who agree that a good autobiography can provide a hazy, metaphoric sense of a life. *The Woman Warrior* provides us with that.

In "Questioning Race and Gender Definitions: Dialogic Subversions in *The Woman Warrior*," Malini Schueller argues that *The Woman Warrior* is "a dialogic text, one which subverts singular definitions of racial and ethnic identity and which valorizes intersubjectivity and communication" (421). Schueller contends that Kingston's work is a feminist work because it rejects all the forms and frameworks common to much of autobiography, especially the concept of a stable and autonomous self which is central to the "phallocentric organization of society."

In Schueller's interpretation, *The Woman Warrior*, as Kristeva has argued women's writing must, rejects "everything finite, definite, structured, loaded with meaning, in the existing state of society." Schueller goes on to argue that Kingston also rejects "singular definitions of ethnic identity in order to combat the impoverishing stereotypes to which Chinese Americans are subject" (423). In sum, Schueller argues that *The Woman Warrior* refuses to project or use any kind of simplistic definition of being female, any stereotypical vision of what Chinese people and culture are like, and any traditional perception of what Chinese American girlhoods are like.

I agree with much of Schueller's essay, especially her initial point—namely that by incorporating myriad elements from her rich personal storehouse of personal memories, myths, and cultural knowledge, Maxine Hong Kingston avoids presenting stereotypical vision of Chinese culture or the life of a Chinese American girl. Unfortunately, after making these points, Schueller picks up the deconstructionists' gauntlet and argues that because of the textual ambiguity in Kingston's autobiography, *The Woman Warrior* is a useful tool for proving that there can be no shared values, no cultural stability and no cultural unity. Schueller discusses the mixed messages Maxine hears throughout her childhood, examines the ambiguity inherent in the story of "No Name Aunt," and notes how Kingston "deliberately presents historical facts and exaggerated legends as if both are equally true" (432). She concludes that the pattern of ambiguity and uncertainty ultimately undermines all forms and structures that have the potential of providing cultural stability and unity. She concludes her essay:

> *The Woman Warrior* thus subverts all forms that have the potential of providing cultural stability and unity. Myths here create

> contradictions and confusions. Kingston writes polemically as a Chinese-American woman confronting and battling with the patriarchal, white American culture, but she does so from a position that is radically unstable. She writes as a woman, but destabilizes the concept of gender; she speaks as a Chinese-American, but questions racial definitions. (433)

In her effort to shape *The Woman Warrior* into a deconstructionist's tool, Schueller misreads Kingston's text in several ways. Most obvious, of course, is that Schueller argues that Kingston confronts and battles with "the patriarchal, white American culture." As I've noted, *The Woman Warrior* does confront the patriarchal white American culture. But most of what *The Woman Warrior* is about is Maxine's continuous confrontations with the misogyny of her family and the sexist traditions of Chinese culture. To assert that her family and their traditions are part of "the patriarchal white American culture" is to fail to recognize that Kingston's major battle is with Chinese culture. Such a conclusion is consistent with what happens too often when adult critics read childhood autobiographies: they read their adult causes and problems into the texts.

More troubling, however, is Schueller's conclusion that *The Woman Warrior* "subverts *all forms* that have the potential of providing cultural stability and unity." For a deconstructionist, any form of cultural stability or unity is dangerous; it can be used to construct universal meaning and values, which are, in the eyes of deconstructionists, artificial and self-contradicting constructs created by those in power to exclude and oppress those not in power. Yet, contrary to what Schueller writes, the final pages of *The Woman Warrior* do not subvert "all forms that have the potential to provide cultural stability and unity." Rather, the final pages offer a vision of peace, harmony, and unity between mother and daughter and Chinese and American cultures. The forms of family and multi-cultural identity ultimately triumph in *The Woman Warrior*, despite Schueller's best hopes. The final pages, as each of the autobiographies examined do, reveal how it is that children facing significant challenges are able to fashion a resilience that empowers them not only to survive but to flourish.

Kingston ends *The Woman Warrior* by telling a simple story that she and her mother have created together. Brave Orchid tells the beginning of the story and Maxine tells the end. Brave Orchid's part recounts how her grandmother loved to go to the theater. One night, although they suspected that their home might be ransacked by bandits, the family went to the theater nonetheless. To their surprise, the bandits struck at the rear of the theater, and did no harm to them. The family interpreted this as proof that the family was immune to harm as long as they enjoyed each others' company and went to plays. Brave Orchid concludes we "went to many plays after that" (207).

Maxine, in the tradition of talk-story, adds to the story by telling us that she would like to believe that when her family went to the theater they heard the songs of Ts'ai Yen, a poetess born in A.D. 175. Ts'ai Yen was kidnapped by a band of barbarians and forced for ten years to live with them and raise two barbarian children. The Barbarians were famous for using arrows that gave off a high whistling sound. The sound terrorized their enemies. One night, Ts'ai Yen walked out of her tent and heard the barbarians, blowing on their arrows, using them as flutes. The music disturbed Ts'ai Yen; its sharpness and its cold sound made her ache. Yet in time, she learned how to write and sing songs that were about her homeland and her family yet harmonized with the shrill, lonely sound of the Barbarians' arrows. Kingston ends the story and her childhood autobiography by noting that when Ts'ai Yen is finally reunited with her family, she

> brought her songs back from the savage lands, and one of the three that has been passed down to us is "Eighteen Stanzas for a Barbarian Reed Pipe," a song that Chinese sing to their own instruments. It translated well. (209)

The shared story indeed shows that Maxine has finally achieved a reconciliation with her mother and her family. Perhaps Maxine feels like Ts'ai Yen, someone who has spent many years in savage lands, but ultimately is able to return home and sing a duet of sorts with her mother. By talking-story with her mother—and by writing the autobiography full of talk-story and its powers—Maxine shows that she has made peace with the traditions and her family and with the cultures and tradition of mainstream Anglo-American society. Thus, Kingston ends *The Woman Warrior* by demonstrating that she can weave together her family's traditions and Chinese history to create a satisfactory and harmonious position for herself. Early in *The Woman Warrior*, Kingston proclaims

> Nobody in history has conquered and united both North America and Asia. A descendent of eighty pole fighters, I ought to be able to set out confidently, march straight down our street, get going right now. There's work to do, ground to cover. Surely, the eighty pole fighters, though unseen, would follow me and lead me and protect me, as is the wont of ancestors. (49)

Uniting North America and Asia is exactly what her story does. Thus, Kingston reminds us that while the obstacles she faced were created by people of two cultures, her resilience and her triumph were also built from the strengths of people from these very same two cultures.

V
The Education and Mis-education of "Rich-heard Road-ree-guess:" *Hunger of Memory*

The critical reception for Richard Rodriguez's *Hunger of Memory* has been contentious and sharply divided. In one camp, reviewers for mass media publications like *The New York Times, Newsweek,* and *The Washington Post* have championed Rodriguez's book as a poignant and beautifully written re-rendering of the American dream, as told by a first generation Mexican-American.

In the other camp, activists and liberal intellectuals, many of them Mexican-American, have condemned the book as the specious work of an ambitious Mexican-American who denigrates Hispanic culture and challenges bilingual education and affirmative action programs in a (successful) effort to win notice and approval from the mainstream American publishing world. I believe that both these views are badly off the mark, and I am baffled by the significant mis-readings that both camps proffer to make their cases. I am not surprised, however, that both sides overlook the childhood described in *Hunger of Memory* and what it tells us about growing up and resilience.

Paul Zweig, in *The New York Times Book Review*, praises *Hunger of Memory* as "a superb autobiographical essay . . . Mr. Rodriguez offers himself as an example of the long labor of change; its costs, about which he is movingly frank, its loneliness, but also its triumph" (1). Echoing Zweig's reading of *Hunger of Memory* as a contemporary Horatio Alger story, George Will writes in *The Washington Post* that Rodriguez's book

> is an affecting act of filial piety, a tribute to the special bravery of immigrant parents who point a child toward a cultural divide they cannot cross. But this book also is a profound compliment to the

> country. He praises what he has lost, but insists that the gain—Americanization: a place in our public—has been worth the pain. (8)

That Zweig reads *Hunger of Memory* as evidence of Rodriguez's "triumph" and Will reads it as a "profound compliment to the United States" amaze me. By my reading, *Hunger of Memory* provides a much less positive perspective on Rodriguez's life and a disturbing view of the United States. It is a place where, from an early age, a Mexican-American boy is taught that he must turn away from his culture, its language, his family, his parents, and even his own sexual identity if he wants to "succeed" in the nation's public life. Dutifully, the boy does all this. He soaks up all the teachings of his parochial school, the Catholic Church, his middle class, anglo community—and these teachings and his own extraordinary intellect provide him with all the resources he needs to carve out for himself a prominent place in American society.

And yet, although he achieves prominence, his achievement comes with significant personal costs, many of which are readily apparent in *Hunger of Memory*. Rodriguez's story, thus, is not one solely of triumph nor is it a "profound compliment" to the United States. Rather, it is a complex mixture of triumph and tragedy and a cautionary tale for all of us to consider carefully before we prescribe "old fashioned" routes to success for immigrant children.

If the mass media's book reviewers have misfired by reading *Hunger of Memory* as a Horatio Alger story of unqualified triumph, many Mexican-American academics have misfired by attacking *Hunger of Memory* and accusing Richard Rodriguez of "selling out" the cause of Hispanic culture. Michael Olivas, for example, has condemned Rodriguez because he has "traded upon his ethnicity" and criticized programs such as bilingual education and affirmative action that aim to provide opportunity to Mexican Americans (37). Echoing Olivas, Ramon Saldivar, in his captivating book *Chicano Narrative*, attacks Rodriguez because he

> chooses with great anxiety and precious sadness to reject the duality of his working-class origins and his middle-class manners; he chooses to market his existential anguish to the most receptive audience imaginable: the right-wing establishment and the liberal academic intelligentsia. (158)

Both Olivas and Saldivar imply that Rodriguez is manipulative and calculating, that he is in power, able to trade and make choices.

Yet *Hunger of Memory*, without much question in my mind, shows that Richard Rodriguez reflects what he was taught and who taught him more than it shows a manipulative opportunist. In *Hunger of Memory*, Rodriguez appears to me to be more of a parrot than an opportunist. He repeats the teachings of a narrow academic education, a profoundly restrictive religious philosophy, and a community that rejected the potential value of diversity in race, ethnicity and sexual preferences in favor of the purported strength of a monolithic and homogenous culture. Thus those like Olivas and Saldivar who accuse Rodriguez of selling out are guilty, at least in part, of blaming the victim.

In any light, *Hunger of Memory* recounts how the son of Mexican immigrants overcomes the challenges of growing up in a home where the family's first language is not the language spoken by the majority and in a community where Mexican-Americans are seen as second class citizens. Ultimately, the author ends up graduating from an extraordinary university and receiving job offers from the finest academic institutions in the United States. Thus, this is another story that reveals much about how a child can overcome many obstacles. Yet this story of childhood resilience, perhaps more than any of the others that I have discussed so far, makes clear that for some children, the ways that they overcome their challenges end up costing them a considerable price.

I. THE EDUCATION OF RICHARD RODRIGUEZ

Only a few weeks after Richard Rodriguez enters kindergarten, his teachers, Catholic nuns, take the first of many steps aimed at getting Richard to assimilate into the strong Irish-Catholic culture of the school. The nuns, in what they believe is an act of charity and assistance, visit Richard's parents and urge them to speak English in their home:

> . . . one Saturday morning three nuns arrived at the house to talk to our parents. Stiffly, they sat on the blue living room sofa. From the doorway of another room, spying the visitors, I noted the

> incongruity—the clash of two worlds, the faces and voices of school intruding on the familiar setting of home. I overheard one voice gently wondering, "Do your children speak only Spanish at home, Mrs. Rodriguez?" While another voice added, "That Richard especially seems so timid and shy."
>
> *That Rich-heard!*
>
> With great tact the visitors continued, "Is it possible for you and your husband to encourage your children to practice their English when they are home?" Of course, my parents complied. What would they not do for their children's well-being? And how could they have questioned the Church's authority which those women represented? In an instant they agreed to give up the language (the sounds) that had revealed and accentuated our family's closeness. The moment after the visitors left, the change was observed. "*Ahora, speak to us en ingles*," my father and mother united to tell us. (20-21)

The nuns' message is clear: speaking Spanish at home hurts your children, holds them back. Desperately wanting their children to have easier lives than their own and having been taught for decades not to question the authority of the Catholic Church, Richard's parents acquiesce. But in complying with the nuns' wishes, Richard's parents set in motion a chain of events that will profoundly empower their son in the mainstream world of the United States but also will distance him from his parents and his own heritage.

Almost as soon as the door closes behind the nuns, Richard's parents insist that only English be spoken in their home. Obedient son, Richard adheres to their new rules but slowly begins to feel alienated from his parents. Now, he cannot communicate easily with them. Emotions, fears, dreams, and love are hard for Richard to express to his parents in English that is simple enough for them to understand. It is almost impossible for his parents to express their emotions to him. Speaking becomes a struggle, and soon the Rodriguez home is no longer a safe haven where Richard can share his life with his parents:

> [t]he special feeling of closeness at home was diminished by then. Gone was the desperate, urgent, intense feeling of being at home; rare was the experience of feeling myself individualized by family

> intimates. We remained a loving family, but one greatly changed. No longer so close; no longer bound tight by the pleasing and troubling knowledge of our public separateness. Neither my older brother nor sister rushed home after school anymore. Nor did I. (22-23)

Besides feeling alienated from his parents, Richard also begins to feel angry at his parents, angry because he feels that their insistence that he speaks English at home is a way of pushing him away, driving him out of the family nest and into the larger world. Consequently, when he comes home from school, Richard often corrects his parents' English as a way of punishing them:

> The docile, obedient student came home a shrill and precocious son who insisted on correcting and teaching his parents with the remark: "My teacher told us . . . "
>
> I intended to hurt my mother and father. I was still angry at them for having encouraged me toward the classroom English. (50)

This anger at his parents does not, I think, ever really go away.

In some ways, *Hunger of Memory* can be read, in part, as a psychological working out of Richard Rodriguez's anger at his parents. A reader may see such a hypothesis as simplistic pop psychology, but it is hard to deny that throughout much of the book Rodriguez is excessively critical of his parents. He emphasizes their limited literacy, their inability to speak fluent English, their working class values, their inability to grasp American society or benefit from American mores. He writes repeatedly about their limitations and deficiencies. He rarely writes of their strengths and abilities, what they sacrificed to pay for the family home, his Catholic education, and his Stanford degree. We learn next to nothing about how they make their living or what they left behind in Mexico in order to give their children the opportunity to grow up in California. When Richard's mother finds out that he is writing an autobiography, she begs him not to write about family secrets. He not only publishes the secrets, he prints—and mocks—her letter.

While that single visit of the nuns is an important milestone in the education of Richard Rodriguez, far more influential are the daily classes the nuns taught. Richard's teachers are inveterate purveyors of "basic skills." The nuns drill students in grammar and math facts, spelling words and historical dates, until all students know a defined set of facts and skills. The nuns focus on memorization, not on exploring students' ideas and experiences:

> The nuns deeply trusted the role of memorization in learning. Not coincidentally, they were excellent teachers of basics. They would stand in front of the room for hours, drilling us over and over (5 times 5 . . . 5 times 9; i before e except after c; God made us to know, love, and serve Him in this world . . .) (89)

The nuns represent complete authority; they have the answers—they are the answers. The goal of students is to absorb their teachers' knowledge and be able to repeat it when called upon. Indeed, at one point in his autobiography, Rodriguez recalls that when one nun told his parents that their youngest daughter had a 'mind of her own,' the nun meant the remark to be a negative criticism (89).

Throughout *Hunger of Memory*, Richard Rodriguez defends his teachers and their heavy emphasis on memorization:

> Stressing memorization, my teachers implied that education is largely a matter of acquiring knowledge already discovered. And they were right. For contrary to more progressive notions of learning, much that is learned in the classroom must be the already known; and much that is already known must be learned before a student can achieve truly independent thought. (89)

Much of *Hunger of Memory* ultimately serves as Rodriguez's defense of a traditional education, of education as "largely a matter of acquiring knowledge already discovered." In many ways, Rodriguez makes a compelling case for his beliefs. His own life is case par excellence of the worlds that open up to a child who has a bedrock solid grasp of the basics—who knows his grammar, can repeat his multiplication facts in his sleep, and has read more Victorian novels than an English Ph.D.

When he begins his education, Richard Rodriguez knows only a few words in English. In time, his speaking ability improves, but he continues to have great difficulty reading English. In response to this, the nuns place him in a remedial reading class. Here, Richard is required to read primers to an elderly nun who, in turn, reads him biographies of early American Presidents. Each day, this elderly tutor encourages him to read and tells him that books should be his friends because they can open doors for him and show him places he never imagined. By the time Richard finishes the third grade, the special attention and his own considerable intellect have made him a proficient reader.

Immediately, he embarks on a "grandiose reading program," the goal of which is to obtain the knowledge, opportunity, and authority that his teachers have told him books can provide. Richard asks his teachers for the titles of "important books" and proceeds to read every one he can get his hands on. He reads Franklin's *Autobiography*, *The Scarlet Letter*, *Great Expectations*, the *Illiad*, *Moby-Dick*, *Gone with the Wind*, *The Good Earth*, *Ramona*, *The Lives of the Saints*, *Crime and Punishment*, *The Pearl*. His teachers are deeply impressed by the little boy who reads exactly what they tell him to read; they make him into their pet and their model student. Unfortunately, Richard does not understand the books he reads.

After finishing each book, he goes to his teachers to find out if he should have liked it and if so *what* he should have liked about it. When Richard reaches the sixth grade, he decides he must memorize each book's "message."

> If the core essence could be mined and memorized, I would become learned like my teachers. I decided to record in a notebook the themes of the books that I read. After reading *Robinson Crusoe*, I wrote that its theme was "the value of learning to live by oneself." When I completed *Wuthering Heights*, I noted the danger of "letting emotions get out of control." Regarding these brief moralistic appraisals usually left me disheartened. I couldn't believe that they were really the source of reading's value. But for many more years, they constituted the only means I had of describing to myself the educational value of books. (62)

A more convincing description of a flawed reading program would be hard to find. Richard may have learned how one reads, but he did not learn why one reads nor did he gain many of the greater benefits of reading. He has been taught that a book is a consumable item with a message to be "mined." He has learned that books are like math facts:

each has a single, simple "answer." It is hard to imagine that any teacher would be satisfied with a reading program that leads a student to define the theme of Robinson Crusoe to be "the value of learning to live by oneself." However . . .

In "Rich and Sharp Memories of Reading," perhaps *the* most startling response to Rodriguez's book, Jeanne Chall, a professor of Education and the Director of the Reading Laboratory at Harvard University, praises Richard's reading program and the techniques his teachers used. Chall is uncritical of his lack of understanding of what he reads or the minimal personal growth that Richard's reading yields him. Instead she supports his experience and his teachers' encouragement to read the classics. She writes:

> A big part of his success came through his development in reading and writing. It did not come easy and "naturally." He received help when he needed it. He benefitted from the help. Also at an early age he read many books—and they were adult—important books. His motives at first seemed to be academic (to prove he could) and to be like his teachers. (40)

Chall defends, indeed supports with research citations of her own work, Richard's reading program as particularly appropriate for minority children because reading difficult books helps to further minority children's syntactic development:

> Current preferences with regard to the reading education of poor, minority children is for content that is relevant to the children's lives. There is also concern that the books not be too hard. Recent research would seem to confirm Rodriguez's experience in preferring "challenging" books at an earlier age. Such books seem to result in greater growth of reading ability as well as syntactic development. (Chomsky, Carol, "Stages in Language Development and Reading Exposure," *Harvard Educational Review*, Vol. 42, No.1, pp. 1-33 and Chall, Jeanne S. Conrad, Sue, Harris, Susan *An Analysis of Textbooks in Relation to Declining SAT Scores.* Prepared for the Advisory Panel on the SAT Score Decline, College Board and ETS, June, 1977.) (40)

It is relevant to note that Chall's research was done at the behest of the College Board, an institution commonly criticized because its tests are perceived to favor middle class white children (who are much more likely than low income children of color to have read "the classics" because their parents may have read them in their school and may have copies of them in their home). It is, however, more important to note that Chall is contending that Rodriguez's reading program of the classics in elementary school is acceptable for minority children because such books "*result in greater growth of reading ability as well as syntactic development*."

Chall is not arguing that reading these books will help children to explore ideas, nurture independent thought, develop a good self-concept, or engender a love of reading. No, Chall contends that such reading is ideal because it allows greater growth in syntactic development. She is probably right—reading Bronte and Hardy will help children write and speak sentences that are more complex. But the goal of a good reading program should not be limited to the development of syntactic complexity. In the classroom of a master teacher, children read not only to develop their ability to read and write, they read to discuss how their lives differ from—or coincide with—the characters and the occurrences in a book. In the classroom of a master teacher, students discover themselves and determine their beliefs as they read. Reading helps students think about larger issues--who they are, what matters to them, what they believe. Unfortunately for Richard Rodriguez, reading is designed to increase the complexity of his sentences.

Rodriguez himself tells us that, contrary to what Chall argues, his reading program was ineffective:

> I entered high school having read hundreds of books . . . but I was not a good reader. Merely bookish, I lacked a point of view. Rather, I read in order to acquire a point of view. I vacuumed books for epigrams, scraps of information, ideas, themes—anything to fill the hollow within me and make me feel educated. (63-64)

Richard's reading program has not taught him how to develop his own ideas: "I lacked a point of view," he admits. "I vacuumed books for . . . *anything to fill the hollow within me* and make me feel educated."

Beyond developing basic skills, schools need to help children develop the ability to solve problems and think for themselves. Schools also need to capture the imagination of children and help them develop a love of learning and thinking, and all the while do so in a way that helps children develop a sense of self worth and confidence. How schools help all children develop a sense of self worth has been a topic much debated recently. Many have argued that in order to build a sense of self worth in all children, a school's curriculum must include and recognize the contributions of many cultures, and especially the cultures of the students in that particular school. This is a central tenet of multi-cultural education. Richard's school never recognized the contributions of Mexican-Americans or studied the history of Mexico. Not once is it suggested—let alone required—that he read the work of a Mexican or Mexican-American author. Instead, at every turn he is urged to read the works of British, Irish, and Anglo-American authors.

The authoritarian style of Richard's teachers causes Richard to idolize them for their power. He sees that their "learning" gives them authority that his parents seem to lack. Richard wants to gain that authority:

> I came to idolize my grammar school teachers. I began by imitating their accents, using their diction, trusting their every direction. The very facts they dispensed, I grasped with awe. Any book they told me to read, I read—then waited for them to tell me which books I enjoyed. Their every casual opinion I came to adopt and to trumpet when I returned home. (49)

> I wanted to *be* like my teachers, to possess their knowledge, to assume their authority, their confidence, even to assume a teacher's persona. (55)

Because they display such authority, Richard wants "to *be* like my teachers.

The failure of Richard's education to teach him how to develop his own thoughts and his own point of view continues to haunt him through college and into graduate school. Stymied in his efforts to write his doctoral dissertation, Rodriguez tries to figure out why he is having so much trouble. He begins to read educational theory. He recognizes himself *in* a book, *The Uses of Literacy* by Richard

Hoggart. He realizes that his education has made him into what Hoggart calls "a scholarship boy," an intellectual parrot who can only repeat what he has heard and cannot think for himself:

> He sits in the seminar room—a man with brown skin, the son of working-class Mexican immigrant parents . . . There is no trace of his parents' accent in his speech. Instead he approximates the accents of teachers and classmates . . . He lifts an opinion from Coleridge, takes something else from Frye or Empson or Leavis. He even repeats exactly his professor's earlier comment. All his ideas are clearly borrowed. He seems to have no thought of his own. He chatters while listeners smile—their look one of disdain.
>
> . . . .
>
> The scholarship boy is a very bad student. He is the great mimic; a collector of thoughts, not a thinker; the very last person in class who ever feels obliged to have an opinion of his own . . . He relies on his teachers, depends on all that he hears in the classroom and reads in his books. He becomes in every obvious way the worst student, a dummy mouthing the opinions of others. But he would not be so bad—nor would he become so successful, a *scholarship* boy—if he did not accurately perceive that the best synonym for primary "education" is "imitation." (66-67)

Rodriguez recognizes that he is Hoggart's quintessential scholarship boy. He cannot think for himself, but rather can only repeat what he has heard and read. Although he is studying to earn the highest academic degree in one of the nation's finest universities, Richard Rodriguez, by his own admission, "is a dummy mouthing the opinions of others." There are, of course, several causes of this, but I suggest that one important cause is Richard's narrow Catholic School education. While it provided him with strong basic skills, it did not enable him to develop his own ideas. Moreover, as I will discuss in subsequent sections of this chapter, Rodriguez's education ignored the value and benefits of his family and culture, and thus left him isolated. He can move into mainstream culture, but he must do so alone.

II. MISUNDERSTANDING BILINGUAL EDUCATION

Hunger of Memory received much notoriety when it was published in small part because it eloquently told the story of a Mexican-American boy's childhood and in large part because Richard Rodriguez used his life story to support his strong views on two controversial issues: bilingual education and affirmative action. For the most part, I do not want to re-hash the political debate that *Hunger of Memory* precipitated; I do, however, want to look at Rodriguez's arguments against bilingual education and discuss them in light of his own childhood and the childhoods of many immigrant children. How does it help and hinder building resilience?

No doubt, Rodriguez's views on bilingual education generated considerable controversy. But to my mind, Rodriguez and those who have responded to Rodriguez's arguments have generated far more heat than light. Perhaps this is because bilingual education has become almost a referendum on the value of Hispanic culture and the Spanish language. Those, like Richard Rodriguez, who oppose bilingual education, are oftentimes perceived to be unappreciative of Hispanic culture.

Nevertheless, I find it surprising that to date no one has recognized that Rodriguez's own childhood—not his own carefully worded attack—offers strong evidence of the misguided nature of Richard Rodriguez's argument against bilingual education. Indeed, Rodriguez's life story make clear some of the benefits of effective bilingual education as well as the dangers of the kind of English-immersion, monocultural education that Rodriguez proposes.

Richard Rodriguez condemns bilingual education because he believes that the fundamental function of the American education system is to help a child develop the speaking and writing skills that will allow that child to succeed in the English speaking culture of the United States. Rodriguez attacks bilingual education because he believes that it retards a child's ability to master English. He believes that children must check their native language at the school house door and immediately begin learning and speaking English at every possible moment. He criticizes bilingual education because he believes it hampers their ability to learn English and because it teaches children a lie: they can speak their native language in a public place (i.e. , a school) and be a part of American culture. Rodriguez believes that to be a part of American society, one must speak English. Those who teach children otherwise do them a great disservice:

> In recent years there have been attempts to make the language of the alien public language. "Bilingual education, two ways to understand . . . " television and radio commercials glibly announce. Proponents of bilingual education are careful to say that they want students to acquire good schooling. Their argument goes something like this: Children permitted to use their family language in school will not be so alienated and will be better able to match the progress of English-speaking children in the crucial first months of instruction . . . But then, the bilingualists claim another, very different goal. They say that children who use their family language in school will retain a sense of their individuality—their ethnic heritage and cultural ties. Supporters of bilingual education thus want it both ways. They propose bilingual schooling as a way of helping students acquire the skills of the classroom crucial for public success. But they likewise insist that bilingual instruction will give students a sense of their identity apart from the public.
>
> Behind this screen there gleams an astonishing promise: One can become a public person while still remaining a private person. At the very same time one can be both! There need be no tension between the self in the crowd and the self apart from the crowd! . . .
>
> It is not enough to say that these schemes are foolish and certainly doomed. Middle-class supporters of public bilingualism toy with the confusion of those Americans who cannot speak English as well as they can. (34-35)

In summary, Rodriguez argues that proponents of bilingual education are guilty of making two promises that they cannot keep. The first promise is that children who are educated in a bilingual classroom will learn to speak English as well as other children. The second promise is that children who are educated in a bilingual classroom can hold onto their "private" (familial and cultural) identity while in school and then, after their education is complete, they can succeed in the public world of the United States while holding onto their private identity.

Rodriguez's attack demonstrates his lack of understanding of bilingual education. In arguing that bilingual education provides minority students with an inferior ability to speak English, Rodriguez ignores over a half century of research that proves the contrary—namely that good bilingual education programs help linguistic minority children learn English as fast as or faster than immersion programs. In "Empowering Minority Students: A Framework for Intervention," James Cummins states concisely what research has shown about the efficacy of immersion and bilingual programs:

> In fact, the results of virtually every bilingual program that has been evaluated during the past fifty years show either no relationship or a negative relationship between amount of school exposure to the majority language and academic achievement in that language . . . Promotion of the minority language entails no loss in the development of English academic skills. In other words, language minority students instructed through the minority language (for example, Spanish) for all or part of the school day perform as well in English academic skills as comparable students instructed totally through English. (20)

While Rodriguez attempts to perpetuate the myth of the superiority of immersion programs, his private opinion conflicts with the public research.

Rodriguez also attacks bilingual education because he believes that it allows children to avoid assimilating into the mainstream, English-speaking culture of the United States. Rodriguez rejects bilingual education because he (mistakenly) believes that bilingual education keeps linguistic minority children forever apart from their native English speaking classmates:

> Today, I hear bilingual educators say that children lose a degree of "individuality" by becoming assimilated into public society. (Bilingual education was popularized in the seventies, that decade when middle-class ethnics began to resist the process of assimilation—the American melting pot.) But the bilingualists simplistically scorn the *value* and *necessity* of assimilation. (26 emphasis mine)

Rodriguez is a strong believer in the value of and need for assimilation. And, no doubt, he makes several compelling arguments about the need and the appropriateness of a public education teaching students how to navigate the world outside their classrooms.

Yet, the problem with Rodriguez's vision is simply that it is excessively absolute in its vision of a binary educational system where children must be trained to be "American" or left to be "other." The issue is not, as I see it, whether children are changed by their education. The issue is rather how much and how fast. Rodriguez fails to understand that there is a middle ground. His own educational experience was one of total immersion into anglo/Catholic culture. Consequently, a prisoner of his own experience, Rodriguez believes that this is how things must be for all children. In so arguing, Rodriguez ignores the *fact* (and I use that word advisedly) that the ultimate goal of a good bilingual education program is to get children who are not from English-speaking families into mainstream classes. Rodriguez implies throughout his autobiography that bilingual education separates children from the mainstream and miseducates them into believing that they can thrive in America without mastering English.

What Rodriguez fails to understand is that bilingual education is a transitional program; it takes non-English speaking children and, without the attendant trauma of immersion, uses their knowledge of their native language to teach them English to the point where they can be placed in mainstream classes. Bilingual education encourages, even requires, students to learn English in a set number of years. Perhaps Rodriguez makes this mistake because, all too frequently, bilingual education fails in its mission—fails to get children into mainstream classes. (Indeed, in my own city, immigrant parents often fight having their children put into bilingual education classes because the records of the school system show that too many children *never* move into the mainstream; indeed, there is evidence that our schools refuse to move children out of bilingual classes because the reduced numbers would jeopardize available federal funds or leave the school system with bilingual teachers who have a legal, contractual right to a teaching position but only a few students who need their teaching. As too often happens, the needs of the adults outweigh what is best for the children.) But such concerns reflect *problems* with too many bilingual education and *NOT* bilingual education itself. In attacking bilingual education for fostering separatism, Rodriguez misconstrues what bilingual education is. Yet there is, I think, another reason Rodriguez scorns bilingual education, one that I want to explore in the next section of this chapter.

III. ALIENATION FROM FAMILY, CULTURE, AND SELF

As I have argued earlier, the nuns' visit to Richard's home is one of the most important moments of Richard's childhood. Their visit, coupled with his daily attendance at their school, helped to enable Richard to move into the mainstream of American life, attend Stanford and write a book that *The New York Times* would review. The visit also sparked the beginning of his alienation from his parents and his family.

The nuns' request that the family speak English ultimately diminishes Richard's sense of closeness to his parents, his home, and his cultural heritage. This not only makes him feel guilty, it distances him from his father (who never really learns English) and his entire family.

> For my part, I felt that I had somehow committed a sin of betrayal by learning English. But betrayal against whom? Not against visitors to the house exactly. No, I felt that I had betrayed my immediate family . . . I felt that I had shattered the intimate bond that had once held the family close. This original sin against my family told whenever anyone addressed me in Spanish and I responded, confounded. (30)

This sense of betrayal pervades Richard's young life. His grandmother calls him "Pocho," the pejorative nickname some Mexican Americans use for one who is culturally prejudiced toward the United States or who has little memory of Mexican language and culture. One of his father's friends corners him in the kitchen and presses his thumbs into the upper part of Richard's arms, making him squirm with "currents of pain" as he tries, unsuccessfully, to answer questions in Spanish. And Rodriguez remembers that on "[n]ights when relatives visited and the front rooms were warmed by Spanish sounds, I slipped quietly out of the house" (51).

Richard's alienation is ostensibly caused by the loss of the ability to speak Spanish and the concomitant sense that he has betrayed his family by mastering English. Yet his "betrayal" is also caused by his education, by the nuns who discouraged his parents from speaking Spanish, and by his teachers who champion everything Anglo and ignore everything Mexican. In "Richard Rodriguez' *Hunger of Memory* as Humanistic Antithesis," an eloquent and compelling article left unfinished at the time of his death, Tomas Rivera argues that Rodriguez never recognizes the worth of Spanish culture:

> He gives no value to the Hispanic language, its culture, its arts . . . The Hispanic world has elaborated and developed much in the history of ideas. Richard Rodriguez seems to indicate that the personal Spanish voice lacks the intelligence and ability to communicate beyond the sensibilities of the personal interactions of personal family life. This is intolerable. (8)

Rivera's points out that Rodriguez shows no appreciation for Spanish culture or the Spanish language, no respect for Mexico and Mexican American culture:

> [Rodriguez] simply attributes negative values to the language and culture of his parents, who have, as he states, "no public voice." . . . Surely, Richard Rodriguez must recognize now that he is educated, that his parents came from a culture that was distinctly Mexican, and non-imitative, that his parents represent a culture with a singular identity. He offers, however, no recognition of the cultural uniqueness of his parents. (9)

Rivera argues, as I have earlier, that Rodriguez fails to appreciate his parents and the value of the Spanish language and culture. Yet, unfortunately, Rivera is excessively optimistic when he argues that Rodriguez "must recognize. . .that his parents came from a culture that was distinctly Mexican, and non-imitative, that his parents represent a culture with a singular identity." Why "must" Rodriguez recognize the cultural uniqueness of his parents? Who would have taught it to him? All his life, he has been encouraged by his teachers to ignore his Mexican heritage. It will hold him back, deny him the privileges of American public life. One need only to recall the books Richard was encouraged to read and the attitude the nuns took towards speaking

Spanish to understand why it is that Richard Rodriguez has so little appreciation of Mexican-American culture.

A useful counterpoint to *Hunger of Memory* is Ernesto Galarza's childhood autobiography, *Barrio Boy*. Born only a few years before the Mexican Revolution, Galarza recounts his family's travels from a mountain village in Mexico to the barrio in Sacramento (an ironic coincidence since it is in Sacramento that Richard Rodriguez grows up 35 years later). Yet, Galarza's 1920's public school in Sacramento shows far more sensitivity to its students than does Rodriguez's 1950's Catholic school.

Galarza recalls his teacher, Miss Hopley, and how things were done in her classroom at Abraham Lincoln Elementary School:

> At Lincoln, making us into Americans did not mean scrubbing away what made us originally foreign. The teachers called us as our parents did, or as close as they could pronounce our names in Spanish or Japanese. No one was ever scolded or punished for speaking in his native tongue on the playground. Matti told the class about his mother's down quilt, which she had made in Italy with the fine feathers of a thousand geese. Encarnacion acted out how boys learned to fish in the Phillipines. I astounded the third grade with the story of my travels on a stagecoach, which nobody else in the class had seen except in the museum at Sutter's Fort. After a visit to the Crocker Art Gallery and its collection of heroic paintings of the golden age of California, someone showed a silk scroll with a Chinese painting. Miss Hopley herself had a way of expressing wonder over these matters before a class, her eyes wide open until they popped slightly. It was easy for me to feel that becoming a proud American, as she said we should, did not mean feeling ashamed of being a Mexican. (211)

On his first day of school, Richard remembers how his teachers, unlike Ernesto's, made no effort to call him by his family name:

> The nun said, in a friendly but oddly impersonal voice, "Boys and girls, this is Richard Rodriguez." (I heard her sound out: *Rich-heard Road-ree-guess*.) It was the first time I had heard anyone name me in English. "Richard," the nun repeated more slowly, writing my name down in her black leather book. Quickly I turned to see my

> mother's face dissolve in a watery blue behind the pebbled glass door. (11)

Rodriguez is too careful a stylist to add that final detail, the dissolution of his mother's face, by accident.

Galarza subtitles *Barrio Boy* "the story of a boy's acculturation." In so doing, Galarza draws an important line of distinction between his autobiography and Rodriguez's autobiography. Rodriguez has made clear that his education demanded that he assimilate, a process that requires a minority group to take on the characteristics of the dominant culture. Acculturation is less severe; it involves the familiarization with the dominant culture and the development of the ability to navigate within that culture, but not necessarily taking on all the habits and mores of the dominant culture. Whereas Galarza believes in acculturation, Rodriguez argues for assimilation. Indeed, half of Rodriguez's argument against bilingual education is based on the belief that bilingual education promotes the "lie" that children do not have to assimilate, that they can maintain the habits and behaviors of their culture while living in the United States. Rodriguez subtitles his book "The Education of Richard Rodriguez," a shrewd echo of one of the 19th century's most influential autobiographies, *The Education of Henry Adams.*

As much as Rodriguez wants to assimilate into the majority culture, he is stymied by his appearance. He has dark skin and black hair. No matter how many British classics he reads and no matter how fluently he speaks English, he feels he cannot completely assimilate into the American mainstream because of his looks. This reality causes him great discomfort and leads him to hate his appearance and his body. Part of this hatred of appearance comes from the attitudes of his mother and her family. They believe that lighter skinned people are inherently better looking than dark skinned people:

> As a boy, I'd stay in the kitchen (never seeming to attract any notice), listening while my aunts spoke of their pleasure at having light children. (The men, some of whom were dark-skinned from years of working out of doors, would be in another part of the house.) It was the woman's spoken concern: the fear of having a dark-skinned son or daughter. Remedies were exchanged. One aunt prescribed to her sisters the elixir of large doses of castor oil during

> the last weeks of pregnancy. (The remedy risked an abortion.) Children born dark grew up to have their faces treated regularly with a mixture of egg white and lemon juice concentrate. (In my case, the solution never would take.) (116)

Richard is his mother's darkest child, and she is constantly trying to protect him from getting any darker. She has noticed the troubling but undeniable correlation between dark skin and poverty in the United States, and she does not want Richard to take any chances. At every opportunity, she urges him to stay in the house during the heat of the day, wear a shirt if he has to work outside, cover himself with a towel as soon as he gets out of the community swimming pool.

Her warnings seem to have a profound effect on Richard. He tries to change his color:

> One night when I was eleven or twelve years old, I locked myself in the bathroom and carefully regarded my reflection in the mirror over the sink. Without any pleasure I studied my skin. I turned on the faucet. (In my mind I heard the swirling voices of aunts, and even my mother's voice, whispering, whispering incessantly about lemon juice solutions and dark, feo children.) With a bar of soap, I fashioned a thick ball of lather. I began soaping my arms. I took my father's straight razor out of the medicine cabinet. Slowly, with steady deliberateness, I put the blade against my flesh, pressed it as close as I could without cutting, and moved it up and down across my skin to see if I could get out, somehow lessen, the dark. All I succeeded in doing, however, was in shaving my arms bare of their hair. For as I noted with disappointment, the dark would not come out. It remained. Trapped. (124-125)

It is not fair to blame Richard's hatred of his appearance solely on his mother and aunts. The family's decision to live in an entirely white neighborhood and Richard's school, with its overwhelmingly white population and anglo curriculum, may have helped to foster Richard's belief that white skin is desirable. Yet whatever the causes, Richard's hatred of his appearance is undeniable:

> [Hearing my mother's comments] anticipates the shame and sexual inferiority I was to feel in later years because of my dark

> complexion. I was to grow up an ugly child. Or one who thought himself ugly. (Feo.) (125)

Not surprisingly, Richard becomes alienated from his own body, refusing to acknowledge his physicality or sensuality:

> I grew divorced from my body. Insecure, overweight, listless. On hot summer days when my rubber-soled shoes soaked up the heat from the sidewalk, I kept my head down . . . I denied myself a sensational life. The normal, extraordinary, animal excitement of feeling my body alive—riding shirtless on a bicycle in the warm wind created by furious self-propelled motion—the sensations that first had excited in me a sense of my maleness, I denied. I was too ashamed of my body. I wanted to forget that I had a body because I had a brown body. I was grateful that none of my classmates ever mentioned the fact. (124-126)

Richard completes high school without ever going out on a date. Weekend nights are spent reading more of the classics and watching his brother dress up for parties. By reading romantic fiction, he develops a "fabulous and sophisticated sexual imagination" and at seventeen, Richard realizes that he "may not have known how to engage a girl in small talk, but [he] had read *Lady Chatterley's Lover*" (127). When he goes off to Stanford, he begins to go out on dates with women but never loses the sense that he is ugly:

> At Stanford, it's true, I began to have something like a conventional sex life. I don't think, however, that I really believed that the women I knew found me physically appealing. I continued to stay out of the sun. I didn't linger in mirrors. (130)

In a November 1990 article in *Harper's* magazine entitled "Late Victorians: San Francisco, AIDS, and the Homosexual Stereotype," Rodriguez states that he is homosexual and intimates that he struggled with this realization while he was growing up. That Rodriguez only acknowledged his homosexuality in 1990 heightens our awareness of the many different pressures he felt as a child—to be white, to speak English, to be heterosexual. That he wrote his childhood autobiography and *never* indicated that he was homosexual or even mentioned the emotional and psychological conflict he experienced growing up speaks to Rodriguez's tremendous inability to express his true self, his inability to break free of all the norms of mainstream American society that were pounded into his head.

In the *Harper's* article, Rodriguez criticizes homosexuals for their refusal to get involved with the generation's major battles and instead retreating into trivial careers that add only touches of style to the world and thereby perpetuate the stereotype of the ineffectual homosexual "dear." Rodriguez begins the article by trying to generalize about homosexuals. He writes:

> In attempting to drape the architecture of sodomy with art, homosexuals have lived for thousands of years against the expectations of nature. Barren as Shakers and interestingly, as concerned with the small effect, homosexuals have made a covenant against nature. Homosexual survival lay in artifice, in plumage, in lampshades, sonnets, musical comedy, couture, syntax, religious ceremony, opera, lacquer, irony.
>
> . . . . .
>
> Why have so many homosexuals retired into the small effect, the ineffectual career, the stereotype, the card shop, the florist? *Be gentle with me?* Or do homosexuals know things others do not? (59-60)

Not surprisingly, Rodriguez's pejorative stereotyping lit off a fire storm of outraged rebuttals. Dana Gorbea-Leon of the Gay and Lesbian Alliance Against Defamation wrote in a subsequent issue of *Harper's*:

> [From Rodriguez's article] we get no fresh view of San Francisco . . . What we get, instead, is a distorted view of homosexuality employed toward mean ends—ridicule, intolerance, bigotry, hatred. That these stereotypes are purveyed by a man who is himself homosexual doesn't make them more palatable or true.
>
> . . . . . .
>
> We are doctors and lawyers, baseball umpires and football players, garage mechanics and government employees; we are interested in the texture and the substance of our lives; we have little or no interest in "plumage" or "lampshades" or the rule of style. (2)

No matter how offensive others found his article, Rodriguez ended it in a bath of self-pity. He describes his experiences watching his friends die of AIDS and yet finding himself unable to embrace them or their cause. He recalls a conversation he had with his dying partner, Cesar:

> When he lay on his deathbed, Cesar said everyone else he knew might get AIDS and die. He said I would be the only one spared—"spared" was supposed to have been chased with irony, but his voice was too weak to do the job. "You are too circumspect," he said then, wagging his finger upon the coverlet. So I was going to live to see that the garden of earthly delights was, after all, only wallpaper—was that it, Cesar? Hadn't I always said so? *It was then I saw that the greater sin against heaven was my unwillingness to embrace life.* (65 emphasis mine)

The article ends on a cold Sunday in a mass at the Church of the Most Holy Redeemer in the Castro District of San Francisco. A woman calls to the front of the church volunteers from the AIDS support group. One by one, parishioners come forth, but Rodriguez, unwilling and unable to join the Support Group, is left sitting in his pew:

> One by one, in twos and threes, throughout the church, people stood up, young men and women, and middle aged and old, straight, gay, and all of them shy at being called. Yet they came forward and assembled in the sanctuary, facing the congregation, grinning self-consciously at one another, their hands hidden behind them.
>
> . . . . .
>
> These learned to love what is corruptible, while I, barren skeptic, reader of St. Augustine, curator of the earthly paradise, inheritor of the empty mirror, I shift my tailbone upon the cold, hard pew. (66)

This is a powerful final view of Richard Rodriguez, alone, unloved, unable to act. In many ways, this ending embodies exactly what *Hunger of Memory* reveals, namely how Richard Rodriguez's childhood, his education, his family, his community, have ultimately served to empower him as a writer and intellectual but paralyze him as a human being, unable to act, to teach, to interact with his family, even to embrace his dying friends.

In the last pages of *Hunger of Memory*, Rodriguez provides a tableau that is just as compelling and just as revealing of Rodriguez's profoundly sad personal paralysis as the final scene from *Harper's* magazine. Yet before I look at the final pages of *Hunger of Memory*, I want to take a small diversion into a stylistic analysis of Rodriguez's prose as an interpretational strategy that will allow me to articulate what I mean by paralysis.

As I have read and re-read *Hunger of Memory*, I have been struck by three distinct stylistic peculiarities: Rodriguez's structuring of *Hunger of Memory*, his consistent use of a nominal, stative prose style, and his frequent use of parenthetical phrases to give brief but clearly subordinate and controlled speaking powers to "others," especially his parents and relatives but also his own "private self." Briefly discussing each of these stylistic features of *Hunger of Memory* will allow me to explicate further my reading of Rodriguez's autobiography.

IV. THE PARALYZED VOICE

Typically, a traditional autobiography employs a fairly strict chronological structure. While such autobiographies may begin with a dramatic scene from the writer's later life, in short order we are brought back to the beginning of the writer's life and begin the march forward. This is certainly the case for many childhood autobiographies such as Piri Thomas's *Down These Mean Streets*, Claude Brown's *Manchild in the Promised Land*, Anne Moody's *Coming of Age in Mississippi*, Richard Wright's *Black Boy*, Russell Baker's *Growing Up*, Annie Dillard's *An American Childhood*, Gary Soto's *Living Up the Street*, Ernesto Galarza's *Barrio Boy*, Jade Snow Wong's *Fifth Chinese Daughter*, to name only a few titles. We have seen this pattern in Tobias Wolff's *This Boy's Life* and in Maya Angelou's *I Know Why the Caged Bird Sings*. Richard Rodriguez, however, does not follow this chronological ordering at all.

Rodriguez's autobiography is a series of essays that have no chronologic rationale. For the most part, each of the essays explores an institution that profoundly affected Rodriguez's life ("Achievement of Desire" is about Richard's schooling, "Credo" is about his relationship with the Catholic Church, "Complexion" is about racism and skin color, "Profession" is about his experiences with Higher Education).

There is a general pattern to each essay. Rodriguez begins with a poignant personal scene then progresses into a carefully worded, carefully argued explication of his opinions on this situation, frequently weaving in personal vignettes from his childhood. Ultimately, each essay ends with a re-statement of his position and a poignant, encapsulating scene from his life (the silence of migrant farmworkers, his grandmother's funeral, a conversation with his father). The essays tend to be circular; the opinion stated in the beginning is restated at the end. And the scenes described show no chronological order: the scene that begins an essay may be from Richard's high school years and the scene that closes the essay may be from his grade school years.

Hunger of Memory is an intellectual autobiography, an autobiography that describes *not* the day-to-day life of a Mexican-American boy but rather the development of the mind of a Mexican American adult, an explication of why Richard Rodriguez thinks the way he thinks. When we read *Manchild in the Promised Land*, *Living Up the Street*, or *Down These Mean Streets*, we experience action: trying out for a baseball team, robbing a store, applying for a job. When we read *Hunger of Memory*, we read ideas about institutions and forces in American public life: education, racism, the Catholic Church, universities. Rodriguez supports these ideas with his personal experiences, but what is highlighted are not those experiences but his ideas. This is precisely why so much of the critical reception of Rodriguez's book has revolved around political diatribes about affirmative action and bilingual education.

This leads me to my next point, which is simply to recognize that because Rodriguez is writing about ideas it is entirely appropriate that his prose style, unlike Angelou and Wolff, is not active but passive, stative and nominal. In "Quantities of Qualities: Nominal Style and the Novel," Carey McIntosh argues:

> One of the most important of general indexes of style is the degree to which the language of a given passage entrusts meaning to nouns and verbs. In a nominal prose style, nouns and noun phrases predominate; what counts is not action, which is so far as possible diluted or hidden or masked, but *relationships* between things or qualities. Nominal sentences rely on being verbs and stative verbs;

> they express meaning in terms of static conditions variously arranged and distributed. (139)

Much of Rodriguez's prose is strongly nominal; sentences "rely" on being verbs and stative verbs and express meaning in terms of static conditions. This observation is not meant to serve as negative criticism. White and Strunk have taught generations of high school students to "USE ACTIVE VERBS." Yet, Rodriguez is describing ideas and states of being, so stative verbs are appropriate precisely because they focus attention on ideas and states, not on actions and actors. Indeed, in the article cited above, McIntosh goes on to argue that "[o]ne of the special strengths of nominal prose is its capacity to make fine moral and psychological discriminations." He concludes that . . . since nominal syntax provides a framework for "dealing" with abstractions, it may be very useful to a writer who is trying to sort out states of consciousness" (141).

After the nuns visit the Rodriguez home, Rodriguez tries to describe how much quieter their home became as each family struggled to speak English. Rodriguez argues that eventually "voices at home at last punctured sad confusion" and there came moments when he heard himself addressed again, now in English, as an intimate:

> Such moments *were* never again as raucous with sound as past times *had been* when we *had* private Spanish to use. Our English-speaking house *was never to be* as noisy as our Spanish-speaking house *had been*. Intimate moments *were* usually soft moments of sound. My mother *was* in the dining room while I did my homework nearby. And she looked over at me. Smiled. Said something—her words said nothing very important. But her voice sounded to tell me (We *are* together.) I *was* her son. (23)

I have highlighted the stative verbs; they dominate the passage and establish a mood, a state. Let me now re-write Rodriguez in dynamic, active prose:

> We never made as much noise as we used to. We used to shout and cheer, laugh and taunt. But when we spoke English, we whispered and talked softly. My mother worked in the dining room while I did my homework . . .

The focus here quickly shifts to the family and the things they did, the shouting and cheering, laughing and taunting. Foregrounded is the action and backgrounded is the sense of silence and the larger *idea* of the cost of speaking English.

Let me play with another passage from *Hunger of Memory*. This passage comes a few pages before the one cited above. Rodriguez is mulling over the changes brought about by the use of English at home:

> But the special feeling of closeness at home was diminished by then. Gone *was* the desperate urgent, intense feeling of being at home; rare *was* the experience of feeling myself individualized by family intimates. We *remained* a loving family, but one greatly changed. {We *were*} No longer so close; {We *were*} no longer bound tight by the pleasure and troubling knowledge of our public separateness. Neither my older brother nor sister rushed home after school anymore. Nor did I. When I arrived home there *would often be* neighborhood kids in the house. Or the house *would be* empty of sounds. (22-23)

Notice first how much focus is put on "feeling." The word is used three times in the first three sentences of the paragraph. This is a paragraph about a state of being. Again, stative verbs predominate (though I admit that I have taken the liberty to add the unstated but understood "were" in the fourth and fifth sentences). Notice the next to last sentence focus on kids "being" in the house (and not on what they did in the house.) Notice that in the last sentence, Rodriguez writes that the house "would be empty of sounds" rather than writing, for example, "Silence embraced me when I walked through our front door; my mother silently chopped onions in the kitchen and my father mulled over the evening newspaper." Rodriguez's prose offers a sense of the mood of the house, not the action that took place.

I have cited only two short passages from *Hunger of Memory*; another reader could refute my argument by citing two passages that are active. Nevertheless, I consistently find that Rodriguez uses nominal prose to express his ideas and his intellectual development. A lengthy analysis of the entire work would substantiate my contention that Rodriguez uses a stative, nominal style that is the antithesis of Wolff and Angelou.

Finally, I want to draw some attention to Rodriguez's frequent use of parenthesis. Far more than *any* other childhood autobiography that I have read, Rodriguez uses parenthetical comments. Sometimes these comments are for clarification, but more often he uses parenthesis to present the spoken comments of his family members, particularly his parents. We thus hear brief snippets of their voices as a counterpoint to his thinking. An example:

> By the time I was born, my father worked at "clean" jobs. For a time, he was a janitor at a fancy department store. ("Easy work; the machines do it all.") Later he became a dental technician. ("Simple.") But by then, he was pessimistic about the ultimate meaning of work and the possibility of ever escaping its claims. In some of my earliest memories of him, my father already seems aged by fatigue. (He has never really grown old like my mother.) From boyhood to manhood, I have remembered him in a single image: seated, asleep on the sofa. his head thrown back in a hideous corpselike grin, the evening newspaper spread out before him. "But look at all you've accomplished," his best friend said to him once. My father said nothing. Only smiled. (56)

Thus, here and throughout *Hunger of Memory,* Rodriguez allows his parents to speak, but only in parent-thesis. It is much in vogue to discuss how certain texts marginalize certain experiences. Rodriguez parenthesizes his parents, and in so doing marginalizes their voice and their experience. Rarely does he present a long conversation with his parents that presents their voices. And almost always he presents his parents in a negative light. Reread the passage above and imagine his parents' reaction. (Note, too, that the passage follows the style I've described: stative verbs predominate and the emphasis is on ideas, not action). In sum, Rodriguez's structure and style enable him to achieve his goal of writing about ideas and education and highlight his intellectual prowess, but the story that he tells, as we will see one more time in the final segment below, shows that his education allowed him to write and make a good living, but it does not let him "love well."

V. THE TRIUMPH AND TRAGEDY OF RICHARD RODRIGUEZ

The final two chapters of *Hunger of Memory* demonstrate both the resilience and the damage inflicted by Richard Rodriguez's childhood and education. In the penultimate essay, "Profession," Rodriguez describes how after he finished his doctorate, he was offered outstanding jobs at several of the nation's most prestigious universities. Yet, Rodriguez refuses all the jobs offered to him. He does so because he believes that they are being offered because of affirmative action and because the universities feel he would bring needed diversity to their campuses. Rodriguez feels that his middle class Catholic education has not prepared him to bring diversity to a campus. "I cannot claim to represent socially disadvantaged Mexican-Americans," he tells the universities. He refuses them all and retreats to a one room apartment in San Francisco where he can meditate about his childhood and begin writing *Hunger of Memory*.

Rodriguez's decision reflects the deep sense of guilt and lack of self confidence that his education and childhood created. With *Hunger of Memory* as evidence, it is easy to understand why universities wanted to hire Richard Rodriguez. His personal experience, iconoclastic opinions, and exceptional writing ability make him a unique and highly qualified scholar, one with abilities that his fellow graduate students simply did not have. He would not "represent" the viewpoint of all Mexican-Americans, but he would bring different ideas to a campus. He is an ideal candidate, but somehow he believes he is not worthy.

And in the final pages of *Hunger of Memory*, Rodriguez presents an even sadder statement of the negative impact his education has had. He describes a recent Christmas dinner at his parents' home. His brother and sister are there with their spouses and children. Richard comes alone, unable or unwilling to bring a companion. His brother and sister discuss their lives and their careers. Richard cannot talk about his teaching, for he refused all his offers. He never mentions anything about his personal life; indeed, he is so secretive that his mother calls him "Mr. Secrets." When his sister asks him what he is doing, he changes the subject. But as he does so, he notices that the suggestion that he is writing a book makes his mother nervous; she has written him before, begging him not to betray the family's private life.

A few moments before, Rodriguez notices that his mother seems lonely. "She does not know how or where to join in when her children are talking about Woody Allen movies or real estate tax laws or somebody's yoga class" (191). Eventually, she breaks her silence and recounts the most recent family happenings. Yet, as Rodriguez's prose reveals, he has long since lost touch with these people and has little idea who they are and even less interest in their lives:

> My mother interrupts. She speaks and gets everyone's attention. Some cousin of ours is getting married next month. (Already.) And some other relative is now the mother of a nine pound baby boy. (Already?) And some relative's son is graduating from college this year. (We haven't seen him since he was five.) And somebody else, an aunt, is retiring from her job in that candy store. (193)

Richard notices that throughout the night his father is generally silent, unable to follow the rapidly spoken conversation in English. The children give their parents "useless and slightly ludicrous gifts—airplane tickets to places they haven't the energy or the desire to visit." Finally it is time for all to leave. Richard realizes that his mother seems sad. He tries to comfort her, but she tells him to take a coat to his father who is standing in the driveway, waving goodbye to Richard's sister:

> I take it to my father and place it on him. In that instant I feel the thinness of his arms. He turns. He asks if I am going home now too. It is, I realize, the only thing he has said to me all evening. (195)

So ends *Hunger of Memory*. Without a companion he can bring to Christmas dinner, unwilling to teach at a university, alienated from his mother, his father, and his entire extended family, Richard Rodriguez prepares to return to his tiny apartment where he will continue to write the book that his mother fears and that argues that his is the right path for children like him. His childhood and his education have given him the strength and the ability to make a fine living. He is clearly a resilient child; he has overcome the difficulties of being Mexican-American in an Anglo dominated community, being homosexual in a heterosexual dominated culture, being a native Spanish speaker in a nation controlled by native English speakers. His total assimilation has earned him almost limitless opportunities to teach, to write, to speak, but it has not given him a life he can share with his family, university students, or a lover. He suffers from his education and his mis-education.

VI
Big Brother, Little Brother: *Brothers and Keepers*

According to its cover, John Edgar Wideman's autobiography *Brothers and Keepers* offers an excellent opportunity to re-examine the nature-nurture argument. The cover tells us that John Wideman and his youngest brother, Robby, "were raised by the same parents in the same environment—the Black ghetto of Homewood, in Pittsburgh, Pennsylvania." Yet John became college professor and a prize winning novelist while Robby was sentenced to life in prison for his part in a murder. Thus, the cover lures readers into Wideman's text by promising answers to a question that most parents wonder: how can children raised by the same parents be so different from each other?

Brothers and Keepers offers no simple answer to that question. Instead, Wideman's autobiography painfully and painstakingly reveals how the development of John and Robby's diametrically opposed identities was the result of an exceedingly complex mix of genetics and chance, fate and family, neighborhoods and communities, people and places. Untangling and examining the different forces that affected their childhoods will be a primary goal of this chapter. Central to this will be a careful examination of John and Robby's relationship, their brotherhood. As we look at this relationship, we will see how much John and Robby shaped each other, how much each brother determined the identity and the fate of the other.

In the pages that follow, I will, as I've done in the preceding chapters, pay special attention to the forces that affected their childhoods. I will try to understand what supported John and allowed him to live a full and fruitful life and try to understand what wasn't there for Robby and why it is that he will spend all of his life behind bars. In some ways, John and Robby should offer unique perspective on the question of what forces help children to thrive. Many of the variables in their lives—family, parents, community—were the same. Yet the culmination of their childhoods could hardly be more different.

I will also pay special attention to the voices that John Wideman uses to tell this story. John Wideman weaves together two voices, one that represents his brother and a wholly different one that represents himself. The voice that presents his own point of view is refined, intellectual, and at times surprisingly dispassionate. The voice that presents his brother's point of view is a scrappy, fiercely proud voice that violates many of the rules so carefully followed by those who like John were educated at Ivy League universities. John Wideman plays one voice off of the other, creating what at first reading seems to be a fascinating dialogue between brothers. Yet, on second reading, it becomes apparent that this is a monologue written by John. He shapes, edits, and controls everything that his brother tries to say. More important, in creating Robby's voice and then controlling what it says, John re-creates the problematic relationship he had with Robby during their childhood. In *Brothers and Keepers*, John again dominates his brother. Thus, by looking at the voice that speaks in *Brothers and Keepers* we can gain insight into why one brother "became a university professor and a prize-winning novelist" while his brother "was sentenced to life in prison."

I. BIG BROTHER

In February of 1976, Robby Wideman was arrested and charged with first degree murder for his involvement in a botched hold-up that resulted in the murder of a car dealer. After Robby's arrest, John Wideman decided that he needed to reconnect with his brother in order to try to understand why this happened and what he might do to help Robby. Ten years older than Robby, John had lost touch with his youngest brother a long time ago and had not had a prolonged conversation with him in a decade. John begins to visit his brother in prison.

As he talks to Robby, John realizes that the answer to how Robby got into such a mess is exceedingly complex. Yet central to the answer is Robby's belief that he needed to "be his own person"—establish his own distinct identity wholly different from John's identity and wholly different from the rest of the members of the Wideman family. In a conversation that John later transcribed into the exact words below, John reports that Robby told him:

> Me and trouble hooked up. See, it was a question of being somebody. Being my own person. Like youns had sports and good grades sewed up. Wasn't nothing I could do in school or sports that youns hadn't done already. People said, Here comes another Wideman. He's gon be a good student like his brothers and sister. That's the way it was spozed to be. I was another Wideman, the last one, the baby, and everybody knew how I was spozed to act. But something inside me said no. Didn't want to be like the rest of youns. Me, I had to be a rebel. Had to get out from under youns' good grades and do. Way back then I decided I wanted to be a star. I wanted to make it big. My way. I wanted the glamour. I wanted to sit high up.
>
> Figured out school and sports wasn't the way. I got to thinking my brothers and sister was squares. Loved youall but wasn't no room left for me. Had to figure out a new territory. I had to be a rebel. (85)

Robby's belief that he had to be a rebel, had to figure out new territory, are critical to understanding his story. Yet before looking more carefully at Robby's story, I want to look at John's story, some of which is not included in *Brothers and Keepers*. Only by understanding each life more fully can we understand both lives—and what they can inform us about the lives of children.

John's childhood was full of the kind of academic and athletic success that adults always praise and reward. Just as John was about to enter adolescence, his father cobbled together a full time job and several part time jobs so that the family could move out of Pittsburgh's increasingly poor neighborhood of Homewood and into the much more prosperous—but barely integrated—neighborhood of Shadyside. Here, John established himself as something of a neighborhood legend, successful at everything he tried.

An excellent student, John earned honors every semester of high school and was selected the valedictorian of the class of 1959. An extraordinary basketball player, John not only re-wrote Peabody High School's record books but also rewrote pages of the all-time record books for all of Pittsburgh's high schools. Gentle, funny, and highly respected, John was elected senior class president and was invited to all social events. Oftentimes he was the only Black student present at private parties in the homes of wealthy white classmates. Academically, athletically, and socially successful, John Wideman added a fitting finale to his high school career by winning a Ben Franklin scholarship to the University of Pennsylvania.

John, of course, benefitted from several of the key forces that build resilience and that we have seen in the lives of the other children we've explored so far. John grew up in a cohesive and warm family. His relationships with his younger brothers and sister were strong—and especially strong was his relationship with his mother, Bette Wideman. The eldest of five children, John maintained a special place in his mother's heart. He emulated her belief in hard work and high goals, and she loved him for it. This is evident throughout *Brothers and Keepers*.

Interestingly, in 1994, a full decade after publishing *Brothers and Keepers*, Wideman wrote and published *Fatheralong*, which he subtitled "A Meditation on Fathers and Sons, Race and Society." Wideman examines his relationship with his father, but in many ways his strongest passages testify to the strength of his love for his mother. At one point, Wideman writes of his relationship with her:

> She was always there. With me. If she had disappeared, no *there* would exist. My world began and ended with her presence. She tucked me in at night, mornings wouldn't commence til my daydreaming, half-sleep haze was punctuated by her feet hitting the floor, her sizzling pee, the toilet flushed, rattle of pots and pans, water running for coffee. If we were separated for some reason, five minutes, a whole afternoon, a rare night I spent in somebody's else house, visualizing myself as my mother might see me was the surest way to make myself feel real. I never talked a lot about my feelings to anyone, but inside my head I maintained a running dialogue with my mother.
>
> When I found myself in novel situations, I often tried to translate what I was experiencing into a story I might tell her. Whether or not I actually narrated the tale to her or anyone else, I wound up explaining things to myself by explaining them to her. She was *there*, like the internal words and rhythm of consciousness

> are there. A closeness and intimacy the opposite of oppressive, since her presence freed me, helped me grow and expand (84-85)

The language here is strikingly similar to how Tobias Wolff describes his relationship to his mother. For both Toby and John, experiences are mediated through their mothers—they write and see things through the mothers. John's description, " . . . I wound up explaining things to myself by explaining them to her . . . ," presents his mother as almost an alter-ego. And he knows, through and through, that she loves him and all her children and her family more than anything else in the world:

> My mother's first rule was love. She refused to believe that she was alone . . . Her God's arms were that circle she drew in the air around herself. Think of circling arms. My mother's arms around her children, her grandkids, her sisters and brothers, nephews and nieces, and inside that circle of family, smaller circles, two bodies clinging, five or six in a tight huddle, circles concentric, overlapping, intertwined, generations long gone and yet to be born connected indivisibly.
>
> . . .
>
> Love the work, love the power in my mother's world. You are not alone unless you let go of love, and if you let go, then you truly are nothing. (51-52)

Here the echoes are of Maya Angelou's grandmother, "a deep brooding love hung over everything she did" and Tobias Wolff's "I could be no one else's son." The power of Bette Wideman's love empowered and indemnified John.

John's neighborhood also contributed to his success. Accepted and revered by his classmates and their parents, John developed self-confidence and self-esteem through their acceptance and praise. The community, and especially his school, sponsored many activities—debates, plays, a newspaper, and, above all else, basketball teams and leagues—that gave John the opportunity to excell, to demonstrate his abilities.

So well nurtured and prepared by his family and community, John continued to win an extraordinary collection of awards from the beginning of his days at the University of Pennsylvania. One of six

Black students in the University's class of 1963, Wideman earned recognition in almost every domain of college life. He won the University's creative writing prize, was elected to Phi Beta Kappa, captained the University's championship basketball team, and, in a stunning piece de resistance, won a Rhodes Scholarship, the first Black to earn that honor since Alain Locke did so in 1907. *Time* and *Newsweek* magazines felt that the first Black to win a Rhodes Scholarship in 55 years merited coverage, and both magazines ran a column on Wideman's achievement ("After Fifty Five Years" and "Scholarships"). *Look* magazine was even more impressed with John's achievement and in its May 21st, 1963 issue ran a six page article on him, complete with several full page photographs (Shalit 31-36).

Look's article begins, "One of two American Negroes to win a Rhodes Scholarship since 1907 is a playwright, poet, prankster, Phi Beta Kappa, and Penn's basketball captain. No wonder faculty and students stand in affectionate awe of . . .

THE ASTONISHING JOHN WIDEMAN

The next few lines recount his accomplishments and also note that "More than one member of the faculty has referred to him as a genius. Girls call him up for dates, professors invite him to their homes for dinner, and soon he will sail to Britain for two years of study at Oxford on a Rhodes Scholarship" (Shalit 31).

To read the *Look* article and examine the photographs is to be transported back into another era, a time clearly before the Civil Rights movement of the 1960's. The article takes on an almost fairy tale quality, a story about a brilliant but poor Black boy who not only wins all the prizes that rich white boys usually win but also is liked, even revered, by the white boys he outshines. There also seem to be two unspoken but clear messages in the article: 1) John Wideman is proof positive that Blacks can succeed in the highest echelons of academia, and 2) that these echelons are not racist—they accept and honor those young men who they believe are "most qualified" regardless of race or socio-economic status.

Perhaps the most interesting element of the *Look* article are the photographs. Most are carefully posed shots, with John playing a different role in each one. In one picture, John, surrounded by his all-white basketball teammates, wears a British Bowler hat and carries an umbrella. "Hand me my bowler, chaps, I'm off to England," the caption reads, and then it tells us that after the picture-taking, his teammates broke into an impromptu chorus of "For he's a jolly good fellow" (34). In another picture, Wideman stands on a stairway with 24 other seniors, all of them white, in the official photograph of the University's honor society, the Sphinx. The caption reads "'I'm the Pharisee of Sphinx,'" he says with a grin" (35). And in yet another shot, John Wideman stands, looking scholarly and philosophic, in the shadow of the University's monument to its founder, Benjamin Franklin (30).

Just as the photographs imply a charmed existence for John Wideman, the text of the article indicates the same. His professors speak of him with awe; the chair of the English department recounts how John received a perfect score on a pop quiz that the professor felt he himself would have failed had he taken it as an undergraduate. Another professor opines that John is perfectly happy and perfectly comfortable at the University, untouched by the racial tensions and differences that most readers would expect a Black student to experience at a traditionally white university. "John seems not to be race- or class-conscious," this professor told the *Look* reporter. "Although he is certainly aware of the complex problems that beset Negroes, he himself seems to be on an eminence looking down" (36). Echoing that professor's opinion, John states, "I've never been confronted with any big problems so far as racial prejudice. I can't say I'm completely unconscious of the problem because, to me, being Negro is only a physical fact. If there were something I wanted very badly that being Negro prevented me from doing then I might have the confrontation of a racial problem . . . but so far, the things that I've wanted to do haven't been held back from me because of my being a Negro. So the problem is not my own problem, not something I feel I have to cope with or resolve" (36). To the left of the article's final photograph of John, that quotation has been shortened and enlarged and reads,

> "I've never been confronted with any problem of prejudice."

—an idea that *Look*'s readers probably wanted to believe during those final, naively optimistic days of John Kennedy's Presidency.

It is hard to know if John Wideman really believed that he had "never been confronted with any problem of prejudice" while he was growing up or if he and the *Look* reporter just wanted to fabricate a "good" story. (It's worth noting that the *Look* reporter was a young Gene Shalit, later to make a career out of enthusiastic excess in movie reviews.) In *Brothers and Keepers*, written twenty years after the *Look* article appeared, John Wideman provides a radically different perspective on his childhood and his years at the University of Pennsylvania. Indeed, in *Brothers and Keepers*, John Wideman recounts a number of incidents and memories that testify to the alienation, anger, and emotional schizophrenia that he experienced growing up and as a college student.

Early in *Brothers and Keepers*, Wideman describes a memory from his freshmen year at the University of Pennsylvania. Wideman remembers sitting in a room with one white and one Black classmate discussing blues music. The white classmate lists the musicians he likes and then, when John lists whom he likes, the white student scornfully dismisses John's choices. "You're still talking about rock 'n' roll. Rhythm and blues. Most of it's junk. Here today and gone tomorrow crap. I'm talking about authentic blues" (30). John is angry that the other Black student, named Darryl, does not come to his defense, and he is furious at the white student's arrogance:

> You can imagine what's going through my mind. How many times I've already gone upside his fat jaw. Biff. Bam. My fists were burning. I could see blood running out both his nostrils. The sneer split at the seams, smeared all over his chin. Here's this white boy in this white world bad-mouthing me to one of the few black faces I get to see, messing with the little bit of understanding I'm beginning to have with Darryl. And worse, trespassing on the private turf of my music, the black sounds from home I carry round in my head as a saving grace against the pressures of the university . . . the choked feeling [of that afternoon] never left my throat. I can feel it now as I write. (30-31)

This experience and others at the University of Pennsylvania helped to create in John Wideman a deep sense of insecurity and self-doubt. Indeed, Wideman is explicit about how this experience helped to instill in him a sense of inferiority: "What hurt most was the truth of what he was saying. His whiteness, his arrogance made me mad, but it was truth putting the real hurt on me" (30). That final phrase—"it was truth putting the real hurt on me"—is startling. It reveals what John Wideman believed as a student *and* twenty years later—that an arrogant, rich, white boy was speaking a "truth" about personal tastes in music that refuted a "truth" about music that John Wideman believed.

Over time, John became friends with the Black student who was part of the debate over rhythm and blues. That Black student came to Penn from Vermont's Putney Prep School. He spoke with what John considered to be a phony British accent, and longed for his blond haired, blue-eyed girlfriend. Yet despite their differences, John and Darryl often left the serene and overwhelmingly white campus of the University of Pennsylvania in search of an environment more like Homewood and Brooklyn, Darryl's home when not at boarding school. Initially, they had little success. "(how could you ask directions? Who in the island of University would know what you were asking, let alone be able to tell you how to get there?)" (32). Eventually, they found South Street. Here, they enjoyed each other's company and appreciated a few hours of not feeling "different" from all the people who surrounded them on the University campus.

For most of the time, John buried his differences with the people who surrounded him at Penn. He excelled at his academic work and basketball. But deep down inside, he was aware that his silence and his role playing were splitting him up the middle, creating a hellish schizophrenia. In *Brothers and Keepers* he writes:

> College was a time of precipitous ups and downs. I was losing contact with the truth of my own feelings. Not trusting, not confiding in anyone else, learning to mistrust and deny my own responses left me no solid ground, nowhere to turn. I was an expert at going with the flow, protecting myself by taking on the emotional or intellectual coloring of whatever circumstances I found myself in. All of this would have been bad enough if I'd simply been camouflaging my feelings. Yet it was far worse. I had no feelings apart from the series of roles and masquerades I found myself playing. And my greatest concern at the time had nothing to do with reestablishing an authentic core. What I feared most and spent most of my energy avoiding, was being unmasked. (33)

Wideman's use of the words "roles," "masquerades," and "unmasked" calls to mind the poses he offered to *Look*'s photographer. His thoughts are a fascinating reworking of how Richard Rodriguez remembers elementary school. Rodriguez recollects his desire to fill his "hollows" with his teachers' knowledge, while Wideman remembers his attempts to take on his environment's "emotional and intellectual coloring." Like Richard Rodriguez, John wants to be like his teachers and fellow students. He has "no feelings apart from the series of roles and masquerades" he is playing, and like Rodriguez, who feels a need to fill the hollow within himself, Wideman feels a "yawning emptiness at the center of my being" (33).

In another passage from *Brothers and Keepers*, Wideman abandons the mask and masquerade imagery and describes his childhood experiences as an attempt to create a protective shell around himself. Yet as he protects himself with his shell, he loses touch with himself:

> The trouble with this survival mechanism was the time and energy expended on upkeep of the shell. The brighter, harder, more convincing and impenetrable the shell became, the more I lost touch with the inner sanctuary where I was supposed to be hiding. It was no more accessible to me than it was to the people I intended to keep out. Inside was a breeding ground for rage, hate, dreams of vengeance. (32)

In an even more disturbing metaphoric foray, Wideman compares his experiences and emotional state while at the University of Pennsylvania to that of an antelope he once saw while hunting:

> Once, in Wyoming, I saw a gut-shot antelope. A bullet had dropped the animal abruptly to its knees. It waggled to its feet again, tipsy, dazed. Then it seemed to hear death, like a prairie fire crackling through the sagebrush at its heels. The antelope bolted, a flat-out bounding sprint, trailing guts like streamers from its low-slung pot-belly. I was running that hard, that fast, but without the antelope's blessed ignorance. I knew I was coming apart. (33)

Wearing masks, building a shell, running like a gut-shot antelope—whatever metaphor John Wideman uses to describe his internal emotional state while in school—all are frightening and have no similarity whatsoever to the portrait presented in *Look* magazine. Rather, all have some resonance with a few recently published books, primarily autobiographies, that describe the experiences of minority students who enter into the recognized elite universities and prep schools that heretofore had admitted only white students.

Of course, Richard Rodriguez's *Hunger of Memory* offers one perspective of being a minority student in elite institutions such as Stanford and Berkeley. But, as I described in an earlier chapter, Rodriguez's focus is not on the inherent problems that those institutions create for minority students, but rather on the deficiencies of minority students and the problems that minority students pose for elite institutions. A better example of what I have in mind is Lorene Cary's autobiography *Black Ice*. *Black Ice* recounts the two difficult years Cary spent at St. Paul's School, the prep school of choice for the children of New England's wealthiest families. The persistent insensitivity—bordering on ignorance—of St. Paul's students, teachers and administrators make Cary's years at St. Paul's frustrating and lonely. Her conflicting emotions of alienation and anger mirror Wideman's feelings about his experience at the University of Pennsylvania.

While *Black Ice* is a useful counterpoint to *Brothers and Keepers*, an even more useful and thought-provoking book is Robert Sam Anson's *Best Intentions*. In *Best Intentions*, Anson tries to understand the tragic death of Edmund Perry. Perry, a 1985 Black graduate of the illustrious Philips Exeter Academy, had been awarded a full scholarship to Stanford. Yet during the summer before he enrolled at Stanford, Perry was shot and killed by an undercover New York City policemen whom Perry and a friend had repeatedly punched in the head as they tried to rob him. Anson, a reporter for *Newsweek*, interviews scores of people and slowly pieces together the many pressures that built up inside Perry. Anson's descriptions of the alienation and anxiety that Perry had to endure at Exeter echo, remarkably, Wideman's descriptions of his days at the University of Pennsylvania. Yet Anson's ultimate "answer" to the question of why Edmund Perry died is deeply unsatisfactory.

Anson mistakes Perry's limited drug use at Exeter as the cause of his trouble rather than see that it was the pressure of trying to negotiate between the world of Phillips Exeter and Harlem that led

Edmund Perry to make decisions that would ultimately cost him his life. Edmund Perry could have written his own version of Wideman's hellish schizophrenia. One need only read a few of the many comments of Perry's teachers and Michael Forrestal, president of Exeter's Board of Trustees, to see just how alone and misunderstood Edmund Perry was while at Exeter (99-106). That Anson—a journalist at one of America's premiere newsmagazines who frequently writes about national issues and trends—fails to see Exeter's complicity in Perry's death makes *Best Intentions* offer not the answer to the questions about why Edmund Perry died. Instead, Anson's book offers further evidence that there will be more tragedies like that of Edmund Perry—and Robby Wideman.

Taken as a triumvirate, *Brothers and Keepers*, *Black Ice*, and *Best Intentions* offer insight about the lives of Black children who enter predominately white elite schools. These three books have much to tell teachers and administrators of these schools. But ultimately, *Black Ice* and *Best Intentions* are about life at St. Paul's and Exeter, whereas *Brothers and Keepers* is not so much about life at the University of Pennsylvania as it is about the relationship between two brothers, John and Robby Wideman. To be sure, their relationship is affected by John and Robby's experiences in school. But *Brothers and Keepers* is about a lot more than school, and thus I want to now turn to a closer look at the dynamics of Robby and John's relationship as brothers and shapers of each other's identity.

II. LITTLE BROTHER

All the years that Robby Wideman was growing up, his oldest brother John was placed on a pedestal. When John came home from college, Mrs. Wideman told Robby to get his haircut and clean up his room. Yet when he got back to Pittsburgh, John spent his time in the kitchen, talking to his mother and ignoring his littlest brother and his friends, who often sat in the living room playing music and talking loud. Sometimes John felt that Robby's friends made too much noise:

> I'd have to yell into the living room sometimes. Ask them to keep the noise down so I could hear myself think. If I walked through the room, they'd fall suddenly silent. Squirm and look at each other and

> avoid my eyes. Stare at their own hands and feet mute as little speak-no-evil monkeys. (10)

Thus, while Robby had to honor his brother, John could yell at Robby's friends, tell them to quiet down so he could think. And John saw Robby's friends as "little speak-no-evil monkeys."

Adding to the pressures that John created for Robby, Robby's two other brothers and sister had achieved almost as much as John. They were successful scholars, outstanding athletes, college bound students. Thus, for Robby, the expectations and pressures were extraordinary. As the last in the line of the successful Wideman children, there was little he could do as a student or as an athlete that would not be judged as "less" than something his brothers or sister had done.

Robby recognized that even to try to follow in his siblings' footsteps he would have to accept their values and beliefs of the dominant culture, and these were values and beliefs that he was beginning to question more and more. Thus, the seeds of Robby's rebellion were sown, as the quotation I cited on the first page of this chapter and here cite again, eloquently explains:

> Me and trouble hooked up. See, it was a question of being somebody. Being my own person. Like youns had sports and good grades sewed up. Wasn't nothing I could do in school or sports that youns hadn't done already. People said, Here comes another Wideman. He's gon be a good student like his brothers and sister. That's the way it was spozed to be. I was another Wideman, the last one, the baby. And everybody knew how I was spozed to act. But something inside me said no. Didn't want to be like the rest of youns. Me, I had to be a rebel. Had to get out from under youns' good grades and do. Way back then I decided I wanted to be a star. I wanted to make it big. My way. I wanted the glamour. I wanted to sit high up.
>
> Figured out school and sports wasn't the way. I got to thinking my brothers and sister were squares. Loved youall but wasn't no room left for me. Had to figure out a new territory. I had to be a rebel. (85)

There were, of course, myriad forces that shaped John and Robby into their separate camps. One force—so evident in the passage cited above—that I want to explore now is called "birth order research," studies on the impact of the position of a child in a family. Reviewing considerable research, Hazel Markus paints a picture of first borns that describes some traits that accurately characterize John Wideman, who was the first born of the Wideman children:

> Firstborns are even more likely than later borns to show some uniformity in their experiences. Among the most reliable—and best-known—of all findings in birth-order research is the fact that first borns are achievers and often over-achievers. They are also leaders, taking the initiative and assuming responsibility. Because they have experienced only younger siblings and never older ones, they are likely to act as if everyone else were a younger sibling in need of their direction, guidance, and instruction. They tend to see themselves as "in charge." And they often *take* charge whether others need it or not, which helps to account for the relative unpopularity of some firstborns.
>
> Firstborns typically have only their parents as models to initiate (sic?)(imitate?) and emulate. This uniformity in standards of behavior and expectations is reflected in obedience and conformity. Researchers at the Stanford Longitudinal Project found that as early as 45 months, firstborns more often complied with parental requests than did later-borns. Sociologist Bert Adams at the University of Wisconsin, reviewing a large number of studies, found that firstborns were relatively more likely to inhibit socially disruptive feelings and to conform to the norms of their group. (37)

Robby Wideman, on the other hand, has several of the traits common to laterborn and last born children: low self esteem, problems with authority, difficulty standing out. Robby (again, and as always, as reported by John) takes on a self-pitying tone and remembers the disadvantages of being the last born this way:

> Okay, you're everybody's pet and that's boss but on the other hand you sometimes feel you're the least important. Always last. Always bringing up the rear. You learn to do stuff on your own because the older kids are always busy, off doing their things, and you're too young, left behind because you don't fit, or just because they forget

> you're back here, at the end, bringing up the rear. But when orders are given out, you sure get your share." (88)

While it is foolish to attribute too much significance to birth order—many oldest and youngest brothers don't follow the patterns the research says they should—the research does seem consistent with what John and Robby tell us about their lives.

While birth order may have affected John and Robby's behavior, family finances, school, and community probably played an even larger role. In *Brothers and Keepers*, John Wideman pays very little attention to what I consider significant differences between his and his brother's childhood: where they lived during their adolescent years. When John was a teenager, his family lived in an all-white suburban neighborhood, and he attended the city's most successful high school. When Robby was in his teens, the family's financial fortunes had taken a considerable turn for the worse and this forced them to move back into Pittsburgh's poorest neighborhood, Homewood.

After suffering from nervous and physical exhaustion, John and Robby's father couldn't earn enough money to make the mortgage payments for his family's home in Shadyside. Consequently, the Wideman's moved back to Homewood just as John was graduating from the University of Pennsylvania and Robby was about to enter high school. Robby thus had to attend Westinghouse, the city's least successful high school, as measured by standardized test scores, attendance rates, and college acceptances. I am puzzled that Wideman pays so little attention to this because it does seem that a fundamental difference of their childhood was the high school experience. At Westinghouse, Robby received an inadequate education from disgruntled and, in Robby's eyes, blatantly racist teachers. Moreover, he was surrounded by angry students, well aware of the inadequacy of their school.

Bette Wideman worried greatly about how the new neighborhood would affect her ability to control Robby, already something of a rebel. Robby, according to John, remembers overhearing his mother express her worries to relatives:

> They was talking about us moving from Shadyside back to Homewood. The biggest thing they was worried about was me. How would it be for me being in Homewood and going to Westinghouse?

> I could tell they was scared. Specially Mom. You know how she is. She didn't want to move. Homewood scared her. Not so much the place but how I'd act if I got out there in the middle of it. She already knew I was wild, hard to handle. There'd be too much mess for me to get into in Homewood. She could see trouble coming. (85)

Mrs. Wideman wanted Robby to stay in Shadyside because of its calm and prosperous environment. *Brothers and Keepers* does not spend much time detailing what Shadyside was like during the 1950's—to a degree it is left to our imagination. Yet, Annie Dillard, in her autobiography *An American Childhood*, describes in great detail exactly what Shadyside was like for her during those years—for, coincidentally, that is where she grew up.

For Annie Dillard, Shadyside was an amazingly peaceful and nurturing community. Neighbors were friendly if a bit distant. Children played in safe quiet streets or roamed to spacious parks bequeathed by the Mellon and Frick families. Fathers made lots of money while mothers maintained homes and prepared nutritious after-school snacks—a world not too dissimilar from the idyllic white world Toni Morrison depicts in *The Bluest Eye*. Every other week, Annie's mother drove her to the Homewood Library, the library nearest to Shadyside; here, Annie read rapaciously. She also saw more African-American people in those afternoons in Homewood than during entire months in Shadyside. She imagines that these people are like herself, fascinated with the natural world:

> The people of Homewood, some of whom lived in visible poverty, on crowded streets among burned-out houses—they dreamed of ponds and streams. They were saving to buy microscopes. In their bedrooms, they fashioned plankton nets. But their hopes were even more vain than mine, for I was a child, and anything might happen; they were adults, living in Homewood. There was neither pond nor stream on the streetcar routes. The Homewood residents whom I knew had little money and little free time. The marble floor [of the Library] was beginning to chill me. It was not fair. (83)

While Robby might have agreed with Annie Dillard that the economic inequity apparent in the neighborhoods was not fair, Robby was not the least bit interested in plankton nets or saving his money to buy a microscope, nor did he want to live in Shadyside. He wanted, desperately, to move into Homewood. To him, Homewood was forbidden fruit, a place his mother always refused to let him visit. Homewood promised to be unchartered territory, a place where he could try to establish his own identity, one wholly different from those of his brothers and sister. And Homewood promised to be a place he could be free of the constant restrictions his mother placed on him.

After the family moved to Homewood, there was no way Mrs. Wideman could hold her son back. John remembers:

> Robby was the rebel. He was always testing our parents, seeing how much he could get away with . . . he hit the streets earlier, harder than the rest of us, partied on weekends, stretched his curfew past midnight . . . My mother's warnings, threats, pleas, had no effect on him. He learned to ride out the storms of her anger, to be sullen and stubborn till his hardheaded persistence wore her down . . . Hitting him was a waste of energy. She'd hurt herself on his hard, bony body; neither her hands, nor her words, made dents in the wall he was fashioning around himself. (106)

Just as important, and again John makes very little mention of it in *Brothers and Keepers*, after the family moved back to Homewood, John and Robby's father left the house. For the next ten years, he visited occasionally and regularly sent money. But the battle of keeping Robby from being lost in the streets was left for Bette Wideman to fight essentially alone.

Neither John or Robby had a strong relationship with their father. Aloof and always having to juggle two or three menial jobs—a waiter at Kaufmann's Department Store, help at rich people's private parties, a garbageman, Edgar Wideman always kept a distance from his children. In *Fatheralong*, John writes,

> . . . I didn't expect [my father] to do much more than come and go like a ghost, at odd hours, to sleep, to eat . . . He was my father and worked long and hard for us. We slept in the same house but at different hours. He was around or not around according to a schedule I couldn't fathom but believed unfair. I learned to accept things as they were, not to expect more, learned as kids must, the

> only way around powerlessness is to make up stuff, to cheat, steal. lie. (41-42)

But it was not just Edgar Wideman's work schedule that isolated him from his children; their father simply never let his children know he loved them: "I was certain my mother needed me," John writes in *Fatheralong*. "My father never expressed such a need" (p. 85). Nevertheless, throughout his school years, John had a father, albeit a distant one, living at home. When Robby reached high school, his father moved out.

And then, the summer of 1968 came. The Civil Rights movement, perpetual violence in the south, major riots in the ghettos of Detroit, Newark, and Los Angeles in the spring of 1967, the assassination of Martin Luther King in April of 1968, and, most of all, the apparent inability of the Civil Rights Movement and the people of the United States to create a just and equitable society, a society that provided its minority citizens equal opportunity and equal protection under the law—all of this contributed to a profound and pervasive sense of unrest and anger in Homewood in the summer of 1968. As someone who had seen, first hand, the tremendous disparity between the predominantly white community of Shadyside and the predominantly Black community of Homewood, between Peabody High School and Westinghouse High School, Robby was uniquely qualified to experience and articulate the rage that such knowledge brings.

In the summer of 1968, Robby got involved with Together, a group of militant Black students who worked to get the Homewood community to stand up for its rights and respond to violence with violence. Together's message was far different from the notion of "turning the other cheek" and peaceful collaboration with white authority that Martin Luther King preached. In short order, Robby's ideas, his ability to articulate them clearly, and his charisma made him the leader of the group and also its primary spokesperson.

Robby got involved with Together because he believed in the cause; he knew how unequal the two societies were. At one point in *Brothers and Keepers*, John reports that Robby suggested that all his trouble *began* when the family moved to Shadyside, and he began to realize that his white neighbors had all the material things that he wanted but couldn't always have:

> Seems like I should start the story back in Shadyside. In the house on Copeland Street. Nothing but white kids around. Them little white kids had everything, too. That's what I thought, anyway. Nice houses, nice clothes. They could buy pop and comic books and candy when they wanted to. We wasn't that bad off, but compared to what them little white kids had I always felt like I didn't have nothing. It made me kinda quiet and shy around them. Me knowing all the time I wanted what they had. Wanted it bad. (91)

That sense of inequality was exacerbated by the move back to Homewood where many children and families lived in poverty and there seemed to be no way for that to change. Robby realized how much of this was caused by the inherent racism and inequality of American society, the difference between the opportunities and resources in Shadyside and the opportunities and resources in Homewood.

Robby was involved in Together because he believed in the organization's goals, but he was also involved in the organization because it gave him an identity and stature in the community in a way that he had never before experienced. Suddenly, he, Robby Wideman, *was* somebody. Not just John Wideman's little brother, but Robby Wideman, leader of Together. And he was an effective leader:

> I dug being a militant cause I was good. It was something I could do. Rap to people. Whip a righteous message on em. People knew my name. They'd listen. And I'd steady take care of business. This was when Rap Brown and Stokely and Bobby Seale and them on TV. I identified with those cats. Malcolm and Eldridge and George Jackson. I read their books. They was Gods. That's who I thought I was when I got up on the stage and rapped at the people. It seemed like things was changing. Like no way they gon turn niggers round this time. (114)

The summer of 1968 and his experience as a leader and a spokesman changed Robby dramatically. When September came and it was time for him to return for his senior year in high school, he wasn't ready to forget all that he had learned. He carried his beliefs and his anger into Westinghouse High School, and when it became apparent that things there were not about to change, he began to lay the groundwork for a student boycott that would demand change.

For all too long, Robby and his classmates felt that their school was racist, dominated by white teachers who lived in middle class white suburbs and didn't respect Black students or understand the world the students lived in. There are many reasons schools are successful, but central to any school's success are two issues: the students' belief that their teachers care about them and expect them to attain high standards and the students' belief that what they are learning in school is relevant to their lives. Westinghouse High School, in Robby's eyes, fell far short on both of these benchmarks.

Robby organized a group of students who declared a student strike at Westinghouse. When the strike effectively shut down the high school, Robby called for city wide action. In a few days they had shut down every high school in Pittsburgh. With pride in his voice, he recounts that history to John, who had never heard it from his brother before:

> Even in jive Westinghouse High people wasn't going for all that old, tired bullshit they be laying on you all the time. We got together a list of demands. Stuff about the lunchroom and a black history course. Stuff like that and getting rid of the principal. We wasn't playing. I mean he was a mean nasty old dude. Hated niggers. No question about that. He wouldn't listen to nobody. Didn't care what was going on. Everybody hated him. We told them people from the school board his ass had to go first thing or we wasn't coming back to school . . . The whole Board of Education came to Westinghouse and we told the principal to his face he had to go. The nasty old motherfucker was sitting right there and we told the board, He has to go. The man hates us and we hate him and his ass got to go. (115)

In a scene reminiscent of Tom Wolfe's 1970 novella, "Mau-Mauing the Flak Catchers," the Pittsburgh School Board listened to Robby's demands and promised to act on all of them. Robby and the students allied with him rejoiced, throwing an enormous all-night party in Westinghouse Park.

But in the end, their strike accomplished very little. Although it made numerous promises, the School Board changed almost nothing at Westinghouse High. The curriculum didn't change, the teachers didn't change, and most of the administrators didn't change. Come the following fall, the major differences were that there were now armed security guards to keep order in the building and a new white principal who never came out of his office.

Mr. and Mrs. Wideman were anything but proud of Robby's involvement in the strike. According to Robby, "All they could talk about was me messing up in school. You know, Get them good grades and keep your mouth shut and mind your own business . . . white folks ain't all bad . . . What it all came down to was be a good nigger and the white folks take care of you" (114). And, to Robby's mother, when the strike ended in a party it only further proved what she had believed all along, that Robby didn't want to work hard and succeed; he wanted to party.

In a disturbing way, Bette Wideman and the family believed in a myth about John and Robby: the myth of the good seed and the bad seed. John was the good seed (from which a healthy plant would grow) and Robby was the bad seed (from which trouble would grow). Early in *Brothers and Keepers*, John points this out:

> Always there. The bad seed, the good seed. Mommy's been saying for as long as I can remember: That Robby . . . he wakes up in the morning looking for the party. She's right, ain't she? Mom's nearly always right in her way, the special way she has of putting words together to take things apart. Every day God sends here Robby thinks is a party. Still up there on the third floor under his covers and he's thinking, Where's it at today? What's it gonna be today? Where's the fun? And that's how he's been since the day the Good Lord put him on this earth. That's your brother, Robert Douglas Wideman (20)

What degree of responsibility the Good Lord and genetics should take for Robby's behavior is not knowable. But, in a frightening way, the myth of the good seed and the bad seed may have become a self-fulfilling prophesy that served to shape Robert Douglas Wideman and John Edgar Wideman. Certainly the myth became a reality, a self-fulfilling prophesy of sorts.

Reginald Clark has recently argued that the labels parents give children, labels like "the good seed" and "the bad seed," may end up deeply affecting children. In *Critical Factors in Why Disadvantaged*

Students Succeed or Fail in School, Clark notes that a study he did in Los Angeles found that "parents had labeled their successful children in ways that were endearing. For example, the parents of achieving youngsters frequently had given them nicknames that reflected a positive role definition. For example, they assigned their children names like "Tiger" or "Wizard," or they would say, "He's my smart one." Such labeling went exactly the other way with underachieving youngsters:

> In the home of the less successful youngsters, . . . [the children] frequently answered to unflattering names like "Snake," "Fatso," "Dumbbell," "Half-pint," "Stuff," "Stinky," and so on. When the interviewers asked, "Why do you call the child by that name?" parents always claimed something like, "Well, I don't mean anything by it; that's what we've called him since he was a baby." When parents described such youngsters, they frequently would add, "He has always had trouble," or "She just really is slow, you know," and "I could tell when she was two months old that she is like her father—ornery. I could tell when she was two days old she had this kind of personality.
>
> And you can't convince the parents otherwise. They "saw it." The question in my mind is, "Which came first, the chicken or the egg?" Did they "see" a particular personality? Was it actually there? Or did they create it? I believe that personality patterns are largely created by parental actions. If the child showed a predisposition toward a certain personality, it certainly was reinforced by parental actions.
>
> I am not suggesting that because a youngster has an unflattering nickname, he or she is going to be an underachiever. I am merely suggesting that labels are often a clue to deeper perceptions about the youngster and about what the youngster is capable of doing. (16-17)

Elizabeth Stone's fascinating book *Black Sheep and Kissing Cousins: How Our Family Stories Shape Us* supports the notion that family myths do more than reveal family history—they shape family history. Through hundreds of interviews, Stone documents how just about every family has family stories—and how these stories about family traits (being lucky, quick tempered, artistic) and about values (hard work, love at first sight, keeping family together at all cost) not only create a family ethos but also shape a family's future. We learn from family myths—whom to trust, whom to go to for advice, and, most important, how to act. Stories retell the past but also help to shape the decisions we make about the future. If I believe that Challeners are lucky or Challeners never move away from the family or Challeners fall in love at first sight, I may make decisions based on that. Thus, family myths and beliefs become self-fulfilling prophesies. How much the myth of the good seed and the bad seed affected Robby and John's life is unknowable. But we cannot overlook the fact that the "good seed" of the Wideman family has gone on to win many of society's most cherished awards while the "bad seed" is in prison for life. And those nicknames were assigned long before Robby Wideman moved from Shadyside to Homewood.

There is, tragically, further resonance to the Wideman family myth of the good seed and the bad seed. John Wideman has two sons, Danny and Jake. Danny, the eldest, has followed John's footsteps—star high school basketball player, honors graduate from Ivy League Brown University, winner of several university writing awards. Jake, the younger of the two sons, has followed Robby's footsteps. He has been in trouble frequently. At fourteen, he attempted to have sexual relations with his youngest sister. Two years later, on August 13, 1986, at the age of 16, Jake Wideman committed murder, repeatedly stabbing a sleeping friend with a six inch hunting knife.

In retrospect, there were some signs that John Wideman's younger son, Jake, was in deep trouble—violent notes found in his room, the attempt at incest, disturbing conversations with a psychologist. But no one expected Jacob Wideman to commit murder. With the benefit of hindsight, some people explained the tragedy by blaming it on John and Judy Wideman, accusing them of playing favorites with their children. According to one of Jake's friends, Lance Rainwater, "Danny was the fair-haired boy," while Jake was always being compared to his imprisoned uncle, Robby:

> "Jake said his parents were comparing him to Robby . . . in our sophomore year he told me, 'It's getting to be more and more each time . . . Every time I turn around they're saying "You're just like Robbie, always getting into mischief."'" (Brown 127)

According to Rainwater, Jake's parents played favorites too often. Danny got a red Toyota MR2 on his sixteenth birthday, yet when he was sixteen, Jake was not even allowed to drive the family's Volvo. When the basketball coach considered replacing Danny with Jake, the Wideman's told their younger son to tell the coach he didn't want to take his brother's place. And when Danny decided to go to Brown University, the family decided to move from Wyoming to Amherst, Massachusetts, thereby making visiting Danny easier but breaking Jake's heart, for he was ready to be the star on the high school's basketball team now that his older brother had graduated.

Court appointed psychologists traced Jake's trouble back to developmental problems, deepening isolation from his family, and, to quote from the psychologists' report, "the re-enactment of a family theme of 'the bad seed.' According to Lance Rainwater, Jake's friend, it's simpler than that: "The blame is all Jake's parents'. I don't think you can blame Jake for being wacko. He had so much anger built up inside him he didn't know how to deal with it" (Brown 128). Of course, it's much more complicated than that, vicious and unfair of Jake's friend even to suggest such a simple and total apportioning of blame in such a complex tragedy. But the myth of the good seed and the bad seed, according to court appointed doctors, affected Jake; it's hard to imagine that it did not also affect Robby. (With breath-taking honesty and palpable pain, Wideman examines Jake's life in *Philadelphia Fire*. As he does in *Brothers and Keepers*, John Wideman explores his own culpability in his son's tragedy and contemplates what responsibility an individual has for his actions. *Philadelphia Fire* is an extraordinary book, but not one that I have space to discuss here.)

In *Brothers and Keepers*, John Wideman certainly wrestles with the why of Robby's situation. I've suggested some of the forces that were at work on Robby Wideman, but one that may have been more immediately responsible for Robby's fate was, simply, the lack of opportunity that faced Robby when he graduated from high school. His high school's failure to educate him and his own failure to get, somehow, a marketable education, his family's inability to make him feel successful and his own inability to draw strength from his family, his community's poverty and his own failure to find a way out of that poverty, all led him to make the bad decision to get involved with drug dealing. No doubt the decision was the wrong one, but there were not many other options. Mrs. Wideman made the point to John eloquently:

> Out there in the street doing wrong, but that's where most of them are. What else can they do, John? Sometimes I can't blame them. No jobs, no money in their pockets. How they supposed to feel like men? (68)

Given the economy of Robby's neighborhood, the limitations of his education, the dissolution of his family, the roadblocks created by the color of his skin, his seething anger at a system that destroyed so many of the young Black men he knew, his own burning desire to be a superstar, his inability to establish relationships with adults who could help him navigate difficult times, Robby had many obstacles in his way in order to become a "successful" child.

Athough John Wideman discusses many of the forces that doomed his brother, ultimately John decides that it is impossible to trace out a precise answer to the question of why his brother is in jail for life. "Why" is impenetrably complex. Indeed, very early in *Brothers and Keepers*, Wideman, pondering his brother's fate, articulates his belief that it is impossible to know when things start and why they end up as they do:

> You never know exactly when something begins. The more you delve and backtrack and think, the more clear it becomes that nothing has a discrete, independent history; people and events take shape not in orderly chronological sequence but in relation to other forces and events, tangled skeins of necessity and inter-dependence and chance that after all could have produced only one result: what is. The intertwining strands of DNA that determine a creature's genetic predispositions might serve as a model for this complexity, but the double helix, bristling with myriad possibilities, is not mysterious enough. The usual notion of time, of one thing happening first and opening the way for another and another, becomes useless pretty quickly when I try to isolate the shape of your life from the rest of us, when I try to retrace your steps and discover precisely where and when you started to go bad. (19)

And while this passage speaks to the complexity and ultimate indeterminacy of "why," it also suggests the inevitability of things, the notion of fate, the notion that given all the forces that existed the only thing that could have happened was what did happen. Such a belief avoids making simplistic assessments of culpability and blame. It also reduces the hope that answers and solutions can be found.

The passage above leads me to a central point of my own reading of *Brothers and Keepers*: that the book re-enacts the hierarchical relationship that John and Robby had while growing up. To put that in simpler words: when he was a child, Robby was often overshadowed and silenced by John. This same domination occurs in *Brothers and Keepers*. Because of his role as author, John Wideman interprets and explains his brother's life. More important, because of his role as author, John Wideman controls and creates the Robby Wideman we meet.

III. THE CONTROL OF LANGUAGE

This creation of a character is, of course, common in biography; biographers create their subject. Yet in *Brothers and Keepers*, John Wideman not only creates his brother, he also judges him and, in a disturbing way, silences him. Indeed, I find that the two most troubling aspects of *Brothers and Keepers* are John's harsh judgements of his brother and John's persistent refusal to let Robby speak for himself. Throughout the book, John not only decides which parts of Robby's story he is going to present but also filters and edits every single thing Robby says. Ultimately, then, *Brothers and Keepers* not only re-enacts John's domination of Robby but also demonstrates the power that those who can command the dominant culture's language have over those who must let their story be told by others. In this light, *Brothers and Keepers* reaffirms the power of language *and* the negative consequences when one person speaks for another.

In asserting that John Wideman controls and silences his brother in *Brothers and Keepers*, I do not at all mean to imply that John Wideman is responsible for Robby's situation. There are, as I have tried to show in the preceding pages, many forces that brought Robby to be part of a murder: a lack of real economic opportunity, an inadequate school system, racism, national social upheaval, divorce and family problems, birth order, genetics, fate—to name just a few.

John's relationship is just one of many forces. Yet, to understand *Brothers and Keepers*, it is important to recognize how it silences and filters Robby, how it offers us not Robby's story but John's version of Robby and Robby's story. Let me move to the text to describe what I mean.

In the passage cited above that attempts to describe how and why things happen, Wideman pulls an interesting sleight of hand. He begins with a "You" that is generic and refers to the reader ("You never know exactly when something begins.") Yet at the end of the paragraph, "you" refers to Robby ("when I try to retrace your steps and discover precisely where and when you started to go bad.") It is apparent that at the end of the passage we are listening in on a conversation between brothers. The sleight of hand merges the reader with Robby. Like the reader in Edgar Allan Poe's "The Cask of the Amontillado," we are subtly implicated in the guilt of the murderer. Wideman, like Poe, thus makes the point that we are *all* responsible for Robby's situation. This idea is central to *Brothers and Keepers*. Wideman wants his reader to realize that unless we all take responsibility for what happened to Robby Wideman, there will be many more lives wasted as Robby's was.

Yet, the passage is also clearly judgmental. While John Wideman may be trying to solve the puzzle of his brother, in so doing he creates a dichotomy between the four older Wideman children and Robby ("When I try to isolate the shape of your life from the rest of us"). Wideman's phrasing is also judgmental; he does not write "where and when you started to get into trouble" or "where and when things got out of control" or "where and when forces overwhelmed you." No, it is "where and when *you went bad*." When I taught in a high school, I had to write citizenship reports for students whom we felt were less than ideal citizens. School policy was that we could not make negative comments about the students, but instead had to focus our comments on their behavior. For example, we could not write that a student was lazy but instead had to note that he did not hand in a major paper and failed all unannounced in-class quizzes; we could not write that a student was occasionally nasty but instead were required to report that a student said things to her classmates in a way that led to hurt feelings.

There are other passages in *Brothers and Keepers* in which John Wideman judges his brother (not his behavior) negatively. Late in the book, John describes his brother this way:

> [Robby had] a basic impetuous honesty that made him see himself and his world with unflinching clarity. He never stopped asking questions. He never allowed answers to stop him. The worst things he did followed from the same impulse as the best. He could be unbelievably dumb, corrupt, selfish, and destructive, but those qualities could keep him down no more than his hope, optimism, his refusal to accept a dull, inferior portion could buoy him above the hell that engulfed black boys in the Homewood streets. (195)

"He could be unbelievably dumb, corrupt, selfish, and destructive," John writes of his brother. Those are harsh words for one brother to write about another, especially to write in a mass market book. In a court of law, Robby would have a chance to respond to such accusations, perhaps even come up with some counter charges about his brother's arrogance and insensitivity. But this is not a court of law. This is John Wideman's book about his brother, and Robby never gets his chance to respond. The only response we get is John's rather weak championing of his brother's hope, optimism, and refusal to accept a diminished life.

John Wideman's occasional harsh judgements of his brother are supported by the structuring and central narrative focus of *Brothers and Keepers*. Overlooking, for the moment, the Author's Note, *Brothers and Keepers* begins with an italicized passage that is, supposedly, Robby speaking:

> When I was a very little child, oh, about six of seven, I had a habit of walking down Walnut and Copeland streets; you know those streets. As I walked I would look at the cars and in my mind I would buy them, but they only cost nickels or dimes. Big ones a dime, little ones a nickel, some that I liked a whole lot would cost a quarter. So as I got older this became a habit. For years I bought cars with the change that was in my pocket, which in those times wasn't very much.
>
> Now this was a kind of wish, but more than that it was a way of looking at things—an unrealistic way—it's like I wanted things to

> be easy, and misguidedly tried to make everything that way, blinded then to the fact that nothing good or worthwhile comes without serious effort. What I'm trying to say is that while I was walking through life I had a distorted view of how I wanted things to be rather than how they really were or are. Always wanted things to be easy; so instead of dealing with things as they were, I didn't deal with them at all. I ducked hard things that took effort or work and tried to have fun, make a party, cause that was always easy. (3)

This is an interesting passage for John Wideman to use to introduce his brother. In effect, Wideman chooses to introduce Robby with a *mea culpa.* Robby acknowledging that he failed to deal with things as they were and ducked hard things that took effort or work. There is no mention about other factors—poverty, family situation, schools, a big brother. This passage verifies what John and his mother will soon say about Robby, that he was *always* lazy, always looking to make a party because that was easy. The contrast between this opening passage and the opening passage to Maya Angelou's *I Know Why the Caged Bird Sings* is dramatic. Angelou, most assuredly, recognized her human foibles in that passage (her poor memory and childish fearfulness) but she also reminded her reader that there were some causes for these foibles (family disorder, racism, and her sense of displacement).

Although he introduces his brother with a *mea culpa*, John Wideman does not introduce himself with a *mea culpa.* The first time we hear John Wideman's voice is in the Author's Note. This voice is full of authority and power. Wideman explains how the book was created. He tells us how he visited his brother in prison, interviewed him, and then "some time later, after I'd had an opportunity to absorb his words but while they were still fresh in my mind, I would reproduce on paper what I heard." Despite the obvious limitations of memory, Wideman defends this method by reminding us that he is a novelist and well trained for such a task:

> As a novelist, I have had lots of practice creating written versions of speech, so I felt much more confident about borrowing narrative techniques learned from fiction than employing a tape recorder. (Author's Note)

Thus, though John never says it outright, we realize that Robby never speaks for himself in *Brothers and Keepers*. His words and his story are perpetually filtered through John's memory, John's point of view, John's writing skills.

Wideman states his ultimate responsibility for *Brothers and Keepers* and establishes his credentials for writing such a book:

> I read many books about prison and prisoners, talking long hours to family members, especially my mother, reviewed court transcripts, newspaper files, and police reports in order to document events and educate myself. I gratefully acknowledge these sources, but also take full responsibility for the final mix of memory, imagination, feeling, and fact. (Author's Note)

Wideman's claim here sounds, in a different but disturbing way, similar to the authenticating strategies that white elites used in introducing slave narratives, as Robert Stepto describes in his seminal work *From Behind the Veil*. John Wideman, like the white elites of the 19th century, controls the publishing apparatus that presents Robby's story. Robby Wideman, like the former slaves, is dependent on this apparatus and those who control it to get his story told and thereby perhaps earn his freedom.

Wideman did encourage his brother to review everything that he had written. But Robby ultimately served more as a source of information and a fact checker than a co-author or an editor. John acknowledges this in his author's note:

> Robby would read what I'd written and respond either when I visited him next or by letter. *His suggestions and corrections usually concerned factual matters*, although his sense of larger issues, of truth and correctness, his feeling for narrative tone and pace, as well as the invaluable quotes from his letters and poems, added immensely to the final result. (Author's Note, emphasis mine)

The net result of this system of collaboration was, in John Wideman's own estimation, that the first draft of *Brothers and Keepers* failed to present a fair portrait of his younger brother:

> By the book's conclusion I wanted a whole, rounded portrait of my brother. I'd envisioned a climactic scene in the final section, an epiphany that would reveal Robby's character in a powerful burst of light and truth. As the first draft evolved I seemed to settle for much less. One early reader had complained of a "sense of frustration . . . By the end of the book I want to know more about Robby than I actually know. I know a lot of facts bout his life but most of his inner self escapes me." (194, ellipsis in the original)

The problem with the first draft, Wideman acknowledges, is that he didn't listen to his brother with enough care:

> I didn't let Robby speak for himself enough. I didn't have enough confidence in his words, his vision, his insights. I wanted to clean him up. (195)

John Wideman thus re-worked the entire draft, "re-read Robby's letters, returned to the books and articles that had informed my research into prisons and prisoners." But, in my opinion, a full rounded portrait of Robby is still missing from the final draft of *Brothers and Keepers*. Robby never speaks for himself.

Another major cause of the incomplete portrait of Robby is, I think, that John Wideman focuses too much of the book on Robby's crime and subsequent punishment. Wideman tries to find, understand, and describe his brother by discussing and describing Robby's crime and his life in prison. Although Robby is in prison, he has not always been a prisoner. To focus the majority of Robby's "biography" on the crime he committed and the details of his punishment is limiting and imprisoning, to say the least.

The great bulk of *Brothers and Keepers* concerns itself with Robby's crime and his time on the road, trying to elude capture. If the central question of *Brothers and Keepers* is why did John become a famous novelist and Robby a prisoner—the most important answers to that question are *not* revealed in the story of the crime. By the time Robby was involved in the failed crime, his fate was more or less determined.

My point in writing this is *not* to criticize John Wideman for writing about the "wrong" things. As a writer, he is entitled to write about anything he wants. My point is simply to point out that by focusing so much of *Brothers and Keepers* on Robby's crime and punishment, Wideman presents us with a whole and rounded portrait of a crime and a criminal and *not* a whole and rounded portrait of Robby Wideman. Perhaps if he had allowed Robby to speak more, especially more about his childhood, John Wideman would have resolved this problem.

Whatever the impact of *Brothers and Keepers*, John believed he had the best intentions. Just after the book was published, Wideman was quoted in the *Saturday Review* as having said that his book had a clear and simple goal: to get Robby out of jail:

> "I want the book to be a part of the motor that might get Robby out of the goddamned place," he says. "I want the book to get all the attention it can because that will facilitate putting his case before the public, giving him an identity other than 'prisoner.' . . .
>
> "But my biggest fear of all is that the book won't work as it's intended to work, and that's to get him out. And that would kill it, no matter what other kind of life it has. It's a book about freedom, it's a book about time. And Robby needs time, and he needs freedom on this side of the wall." (Rause 56)

While perhaps not surprising to anyone who has read *Brothers and Keepers*, Wideman's comment works to undermine a belief in his objectivity and authorial authority. Moreover, Wideman's comment recasts questions about *Brothers and Keepers*' focus on Robby's criminality and John's refusal to let Robby speak for himself.

The publication in 1984 of *Brothers and Keepers* called to many readers' minds Norman Mailer's tragic dance with Jack Henry Abbott and *In the Belly of the Beast*. While he was writing *The Executioner's Song*, the story of Gary Gilmore, a convicted murderer who became the first U.S. citizen to be executed after the Supreme Court reinstated capital punishment in the 1970's, Norman Mailer received a letter from Abbott. A lifelong convict, Abbott asserted that he could teach Mailer a lot about prisons and prisoners. A lively correspondence began. Eventually, Mailer was so taken by Abbott's literary style and unique vision that he convinced the editors of Random House to publish Abbott's letters under the title of *In the Belly of the Beast: Letters from Prison*.

Mailer wrote the introduction to this work. It is surprisingly short but otherwise vintage Mailer: self-aggrandizing, apocalyptic, powerful. He argues not about the injustice of Abbott's prison sentence nor the validity of Abbott's views. Instead, Mailer trumpets the power and beauty of Abbott's prose. If Jack Henry Abbott gets out of jail, "we may yet have a new writer of the largest stature among us." (Abbott xviii.) Mailer then closes his introduction by declaring, "I love Jack Abbott for surviving and for having learned to write as well as he does" (xviii). Every word thereafter is written by Abbott. In the 198 pages that follow, Abbott advances radical ideas about reshaping American society and strict Marxist interpretations of international affairs. The book, and Mailer's championing, got so much national attention that ultimately Jack Abbott was released from state prison.

Why *In The Belly of the Beast* succeeded in freeing Jack Henry Abbott while *Brothers and Keepers* failed to free Robert Wideman is hard to know. The different outcomes may reflect the difference of what happens when a white literary figure champions a white criminal as compared to what happens when a Black literary figure champions a black criminal. Or it may reflect the difference of the stature of the two literary figures; Mailer, the winner of two Pulitzers, is probably the most widely recognized writer of his generation, while Wideman, although highly respected in university English departments, is not widely known by the public at large.

John Wideman's inability to free his brother can also be attributed to the colossal tragedy caused by Abbott's release. In 1982, only months after his release, Abbott murdered a New Orleans waiter who brought him water too slowly. This tragedy must have cooled any parole board's ardor, in 1984, to release John Wideman's brother. Also important is the difference between Abbott's and Wideman's crime; while both men committed armed robberies, Robby's had ended in a murder, whereas no one was hurt during Abbott's crime. Yet, ultimately, I believe that the different in outcome is also, at least in part, attributable to Mailer's decision to let Abbott speak for himself. Abbott makes the best case for his freedom; Robby Wideman never got that opportunity.

While he admitted that his goal in *Brothers and Keepers* was to free Robby, John Wideman acknowledges that in writing *Brothers and Keepers* he was also trying to come to some personal understanding of his brother's tragedy. This working through, this effort to understand

Robby's tragedy is apparent in several of Wideman's other works, especially *Hiding Place*, the third of his trilogy of novels about Homewood. A short examination of these will provide some final thoughts about John and Robby's relationship.

I read *Hiding Place* as more than just another attempt to understand Robby's situation; I read *Hiding Place* as the fictional re-working of *Brothers and Keepers*. The similarities between the plot of *Hiding Place* and Robby's story are exceedingly similar. In *Hiding Place* a young Black man named Tommy gets involved in a botched heist of television sets in which one of his partners shoots and kills another man. The fictional murder scene in *Hiding Place* is almost identical to the actual place where Robby's burglary attempt ended in murder. Both take place on the grounds of an auto garage on the west side of Pittsburgh in the late afternoon, when the wind is swirling and the light is fading. Tommy shares a lot in common with Robby Wideman. Tommy, like Robby, is blessed with the ability to speak, to "lay a mean rap on anyone." Tommy, like Robby, has a son and a wife, whom he has abandoned, a grandmother named Freeda French, and a college educated brother who was a star basketball player and now lives in Wyoming. In *Hiding Place*, Tommy's uncle describes Tommy in a way that mirrors what Robby's mother has said about Robby in *Brothers and Keepers*: "He's still like a child. He always wanted every day to be a party. A party from morning till night. He'd wake up looking for the party" (102). And after the botched heist and murder, Tommy, like Robby, runs from the police.

But in their running, Tommy and Robby Wideman differ significantly. Tommy does not run with his fellow gangsters across the country. Instead, in the dead of night, Tommy sneaks up to his great grandmother's home, a shack on top of an abandoned hill on the outskirts of Pittsburgh's ghetto. His grandmother, known as Mother Bess, is a curmudgeon. She has, for the last decade, insisted on living alone in her shack and insults the few visitors who make their way up her hill. In a beautifully written series of conversations, Tommy and Mother Bess exchange their life stories. Ultimately, Tommy decides he cannot do what she has done and hide from the world. Heroically, he leaves her shack and starts to make his way down her hill to face the police. Before he gets very far from Mother Bess's home, the police spot him and shots are fired. Mother Bess hears the shots and prepares to go out and help Tommy:

> She damns them and hobbles back to her porch, an old woman startled from her sleep in the middle of the night, an old woman in a dark house who knows it's too late to help him, who knows he's long gone, who knows her arms are too week to lift him and carry him back where he belongs (157)

Wideman never explicitly states whether or not Tommy is killed; I read the line ". . . an old woman in a dark house who *knows it's too late to help him, who knows he's long gone*," to mean that Tommy has been shot *and* killed. Similarly, I interpret the novel's final passage as indicating that Tommy has been killed:

> Because somebody has to go down there and tell the truth. Lizabeth's boy didn't kill nobody. He wasn't scared. All he needed was another chance and somebody needs to go down there and tell them. And she was going to do just that. Burn down that last bit of shack on Bruston Hill and tell them what they needed to know. That he ain't killed nobody. That he needed one more chance. That he staked his life on one more chance. They should know all that down there. She'll tell them. She'll make sure they hear. Yes indeed. On her man's arms now. Four good legs now and she's coming. She's coming to tell them he ain't scared no more and they better listen and they better make sure it don't happen so easy ever again. (158)

Despite Tommy's death, I read *Hiding Place* as a more optimistic and life affirming rendering of the robbery Robby was involved in. In *Hiding Place*, Tommy returns to the matriarch of his family and gains energy from her and her connection to his family. She—and by extension his family—empower him to face up to his accusers in a heroic way. By novel's end, he is an existential hero of sorts. His wrong pales in comparison to the wrong of trigger-happy police. How much *Hiding Place* functions as John Wideman's working through to a acceptable conclusion his brother's situation is not for me to decide. My point is simply to recognize *Hiding Place*'s dramatic similarity to *Brothers and Keepers* and to point out how their differences speak to the central conflicts of *Brothers and Keepers*.

James Coleman's *Blackness and Modernism: The Literary Career of John Edgar Wideman* stands as the only book wholly about John Wideman's work. Coleman's work provides important and insightful attention to Wideman's novels. Nevertheless, *Blackness and Modernism*'s pays little attention to *Brothers and Keepers. Blackness and Modernism* develops a thesis: that Wideman's development as a writer began with him writing novels that ignored Black culture and then, after he spent ten years reading and teaching Black literature, his work changed dramatically and has culminated with Wideman writing outstanding novels that embody Black life. In his introduction, Coleman says as much:

> During his career as a writer-intellectual, John Edgar Wideman in his personal life has overcome feelings of alienation from the black community and has reoriented himself as a participant in black culture. In his fiction, I contend, Wideman has effected a similar shift, using modernism and postmodernism to bring his intellectual characters out of their isolation and into contact with the needs, concerns, and traditions of black people generally. Before he could write about this shift, Wideman had to inform himself about black culture. An eight year period of immersion in the works of nineteenth and twentieth-century authors gave him the resources he needed. Using them, he was able to circumvent modernism's dead-end, pessimistic worldview and at the same time to chart a new course for other, similarly estranged black intellectuals. (3)

One problem with *Blackness and Modernism* is that Coleman takes great pains to argue that each of Wideman's novels demonstrates a "next step" in his "development." The notion of logical, step-by-step growth is antithetical to what most artists recognize as true about development—it doesn't go step by step, logically forward. Instead, development comes in great leaps forward followed by steps backward and sideways and totally unrelated. More troubling is Coleman's continued insistence that the transformation of Wideman's prose style is directly caused by his reading of other Black authors. The assertion is demeaning; it makes Wideman into more of a mimic than an artist. It also oversimplifies Wideman's work, as a one dimensional working out of other writers' books and the anxiety of influence. But most troubling to me is that Coleman's study ignores the personal element of Wideman's work. Coleman gives very short shrift to the effect that Wideman's life and relations with family had on the shift in his prose style and his plots.

In his chapter on *Hiding Place*, Coleman repeatedly emphasizes Wideman's debt to other black writers and gives little attention to the impact that Wideman's family and life has on the novel. He also offers questionable interpretations of the novel; he contends that Tommy is not killed at the novel's end but is rather saved; he argues that Mother Bess will go down the mountain and "that will make her a loving caring person again and will enable her to reenter the community" (71). Most disturbing of all is his bald assertion that Tommy and Robby are the same person:

> Tommy, who is the same person as Robby in *Brothers and Keepers*, is part of the 1960's generation" (74).

This is a troubling sentence, for it blurs not only the differences between the characters but also the differences between a novel and an auto/biography.

Blackness and Modernism generally ignores *Brothers and Keepers*. Coleman offers full chapters on each of Wideman's novels, including his 1989 novel *Reuben.* Yet Coleman offers only four pages of commentary on *Brothers and Keepers*, published in 1984. Both by length and by care, Coleman makes it clear that he does not think *Brothers and Keepers* is essential to John's achievement. I, of course, believe that just the opposite is true. I believe that *Brothers and Keepers* is the central work in John Wideman's career. It triggered the Homewood trilogy and freed him to write books such as *Philadelphia Fire*, *Fever,* and *Fatheralong* . Moreover, I think it was Robby's life, not reading and teaching Black literature, that was most responsible for the general shift in Wideman's style and focus. I would speculate that Wideman's immersion in the works of Black authors, no doubt, helped to focus and enrich his writing, but those works were not nearly as central a catalyst as Robby's life. But this is simply my own speculation.

While I cannot determine influences on John Edgar Wideman, I want to end this chapter by recognizing that the influences in his own life are similar to those of other resilient children we have discussed in previous chapters. John's family was strong and cohesive; his mother provided unconditional love. His community provided ample opportunities for John to develop skills and then lavished him with praise and support when he demonstrated those skills—be that in class, on the basketball court, or during a debate. John, in turn, not only capitalized on these various support systems, but he also developed a voice—albeit one that never spoke the plain truth—that enabled him to build relationships and friendships with many adults who could help him. The development of an "empowering voice" is exactly what we have seen in the stories of Maya Angelou and Tobias Wolff, Richard Rodriguez and Maxine Hong Kingston—as well as in many other childhood autobiographies. This, of course, is exactly what Emmy Werner and a host of others who have researched resilience have found to be a commonality among resilient children.

Although he was John Wideman's brother, Robby Wideman did not have most of the resources and opportunities that John had and that typically build resilience. By the time Robby was out of grade school, the family was falling apart and he was cast in the role of the "bad seed." The opportunities provided by the Shadyside community that supported John simply did not exist for Robby in Homewood. The only voice and role that Robby was able to develop was one that put him in jail for all of his natural life. *Brothers and Keepers*, knowingly and unknowingly, offers much food for thought about how children are able to build resilience.

VII
Resilience or Silence

Walking home from work last night, I traveled through an underpass. As the cars and trucks on Interstate 195 roared overhead, I noticed that on the walls of the underpass someone had spray-painted this message: Silence = Death. I walked on, through another underpass. The same spray-painted message appeared: Silence = Death. Feeling like a bit like a character in Thomas Pynchon's *The Crying of Lot 49*, I began to think about the message of the spray painter and how it applies to this final chapter and the five autobiographies we have discussed.

Each of these five autobiographies describes, literally and figuratively, a child's struggle to overcome many challenges and not be silenced. As we've seen, the problems facing these children are numerous and varied: absent fathers, absent mothers, dysfunctional families, ineffective schools, impoverished communities, alcoholism, sexual abuse, physical abuse, verbal abuse, psychological abuse, racism, poverty, and our nation's insistent privileging of rich children over poor children, boys over girls, English speakers over non-English speakers, and white children over children of color.

In each of the autobiographies, all five children reach a moment when they are unable to speak about the forces that are silencing them or ask for help from the people who profess to love them. Maya Angelou cannot speak after the man who raped her is murdered. Tobias Wolff cannot speak when his mother asks him if she should marry the man who abuses him, Maxine Hong Kingston cannot speak after she bullies her perpetually silent classmate, Richard Rodriguez cannot speak with his parents after the nuns insist English be the only language spoken in his home, and John Wideman cannot speak to anyone about his experiences at the University of Pennsylvania. And, yet, as we have seen, Angelou, Wolff, Kingston, Rodriguez, and Wideman all eventually overcome the forces that have silenced them and go on to live productive lives.

The forces that silence young people are central to many stories about youth. My focus has been on five autobiographies, yet many other autobiographies and novels depict how children are silenced. *Down These Mean Streets*, *Barrio Boy*, *Fifth Chinese Daughter*, *Coming of Age In Mississippi*, *Manchild in the Promised Land*, *The Bluest Eye*, *The Catcher in the Rye*, *A Boy's Own Story*, *Child of the Dark*, *Best Intentions*, and *The Education of Little Tree* all describe the life of a child who speaks out. I suspect that a systematic reading of autobiographies and novels about childhood would reveal this as a central commonality. I hope some scholars and some young people will explore this idea.

When I first began writing these chapters, I was directing a community-based assessment of my city's public schools. As part of our research, we interviewed and conducted focus groups with dozens of randomly selected students in each of the city's high schools and middle schools. In the focus groups, no adults from the school or the district administration were present; it was just me and students. And in almost all of the focus groups, students told me—again and again—how much they feel that they no one listens to them and that one of the chief goals of most of the adults in their schools is to control students and keep them quiet.

In one of the middle schools, an enormous fortress that would frighten any twelve year old and certainly frightened and depressed me, the students asked if they could give me a tour of their school after their focus group discussion. With some reservations and after giving the students about five minutes of instruction, the principal agreed. As soon as we left the front office, the students assured me that no matter where we went, we would hear adults telling children to be quiet. As we walked up and down three floors of hallways, I could hear how right they were. Again and again I heard adults tell children to be quiet, to stop whispering, to raise your hand before you speak, and, in more than one classroom, to shut up. (To give the devil its due, sort of, we also heard praise for Aisha because she was working so quietly, praise for the children in room 309 because it was absolutely silent in their room, and praise for Carlos because he was waiting so patiently to be called on.)

Yet, although these students and many autobiographies show quite clearly that there are many forces that try to silence children, these five autobiographies prove that all children who face challenges are not forever silenced. Indeed, these autobiographies tell the stories of children who overcame the forces that might have silenced them and went on to live meaningful, independent lives. Most important of all, these autobiographies and a growing body of research prove that there is much cause for hope—that children can and often do overcome the very risk factors that, according to social scientists, doom children to fail.

Thus, we return to the questions posed at the beginning of this study: what is it that makes children resilient? Why is it that some children overcome extraordinary obstacles? To offer any definitive answer to such a complex question is impossible. But here, at the end of this study, it is surely worth pointing out some of the common forces that contributed to the resilience of the authors. I argued in my introduction that the most important purpose of this study is to think about what makes some children resilient and try to determine what it is that adults can do to help build this resilience. Thus, it is appropriate to conclude this study by trying, one more time, to answer these questions.

In broadest terms, we can see three key sources of support in the five works we have examined: 1) families, especially mothers, 2) neighbors and neighborhoods, and 3) community institutions, especially schools and churches. Each of the children in these five autobiographies received significant support from at least two of these three sources. And, as we'll discuss later, there is a growing body of research that shows that within a broader, more general population of children, these same three sources of support—families, neighborhoods, and institutions--are often central to what builds resilience in all children.

In our five autobiographies, it is obvious that first and foremost adult female family members contributed dramatically to the resilience of all five children. An adult women stood by each of these children no matter what problem they faced. Maya Angelou, of course, had her grandmother. While she was often exceedingly strict and frequently complained of the burden that Maya created, Grandmother Henderson never failed to look after Maya, never failed to protect and provide for her. For Toby, Maxine, and John, the importance of their mothers is readily apparent. Brave Orchid encourages Maxine to become a woman warrior, Rosemary Wolff defends him against all his critics and keeps alive his sense of self-esteem, and Bette Wideman who builds in John a sense of his talents and potential. While Richard Rodriguez writes little about his mother, he notes that, more than anyone else, she steadfastly encouraged, supported, and believed in him. He dedicates *Hunger of Memory* to her and his father.

While women contribute to the resilience of these five children, men either create hardship or are absent from the lives of these children. Toby and Maya are abandoned by their fathers and suffer the pain of this rejection throughout their childhoods. John, Maxine, and Richard have ineffectual fathers; they are rarely mentioned in the autobiographies—and when they are mentioned they are usually described as feckless or failed. This pattern, as I've mentioned before, is common to many other autobiographies about difficult childhoods—*Down These Mean Streets, Manchild in the Promised Land, Barrio Boy, Coming of Age in Mississippi, Growing Up, This Stubborn Soil, The Autobiography of Malcolm X, Living Up the Street.* Indeed, the theme is so prevalent that it begs the question "why do fathers rarely play a role in building resilience in at-risk children" Perhaps some of the answer is that when effective, wage-earning fathers are present, children are much less likely to become at-risk. Yet, as we've seen, part of the answer is, simply, that fathers frequently fail as parents and disappear from the lives of children and cause great hardship.

It is, however, more than mothers and grandmothers who contribute to the extraordinary resilience of Maya Angelou, Tobias Wolff, John Wideman, Maxine Kingston, and Richard Rodriguez. A community of people, a few related but most simply involved because of the happenstance of neighborhood, contribute to the resilience of these five children. *I Know Why the Caged Bird Sings* provides a model of what a community can contribute to a child's life. In Stamps there is an extraordinary web of support for Maya including the church (with its picnics, services, and revivals), the elementary school (with its first rate teachers and strong community support for its mission), the family store (with dozens of customers who regularly complement Maya on her skills and ask her about her academic progress.) It is much in vogue these days to cite the African proverb "It takes an entire village to raise a child." And while this may not always be true—extraordinary children have been raised without the support of an entire village—Stamps demonstrates that, indeed, if an entire village is willing to pitch in, an amazing child can be raised.

I opened this study by contrasting the fate of Maya Angelou with the fate of *The Bluest Eye's* Pecola Breedlove. Perhaps the most cogent explanation of their different fates lies in the differences in the different levels of support provide by their community. Everyone in Maya's neighborhood in Stamps contributed to Maya's growth while virtually no one in Lorain, Ohio reached out to Pecola. (Ironically, through my work in assessing our city's schools, I received a thoughtful needs assessment commissioned by the people of Lorain, Ohio and an invitation to meet with some citizens and discuss what they should do next. What was foremost in their blunt assessment of the community's failures is the recognition that the needs of poor, minority children are ignored and that something must be done about it. Perhaps they could have saved the cost of the assessment and just read *The Bluest Eye* and *I Know Why the Caged Bird Sings*.)

People who live and work in the community support Toby, Maxine, Richard, and John. All four receive encouragement, instruction, opportunities to excel, and praise from neighbors, friends of the family, and a host of community volunteers. The importance of broad community support in raising resilient children has been recently documented in several sociological studies. Echoing what we have seen in these five autobiographies, Emmy Werner's recent work, *Overcoming the Odds: High Risk Children from Birth to Adulthood*, concludes that two of the most consistent variables that served to protect high risk children are effective parents (especially mothers) and supportive communities:

> The other variables that appeared as protective buffers in the lives of high risk children were parental competence and caregiving style (especially that of the mother) and a variety of sources of support in the family, neighborhood, school and community which the individual attracted during early and middle childhood, late adolescence, and young adulthood. Among gatekeepers that fostered trust, autonomy, and initiative were grandparents, older siblings, caring adults in the neighborhood, teachers that acted as role models and counselors, ministers and youth workers, close friends, spouses and mates. (199)

Werner notes that these findings—that family and community can make critical contributions to the resilience of youth—have been supported by several other studies, which she cites.

Certainly, Werner's conclusions match, almost identically, the work of Reginald Clark and Urie Bronfenbrenner that I cited earlier. And the work of all three is consistent with the conclusions that I made in research funded by The Ford Foundation in the late 1980's and based on interviews with students from Providence, Rhode Island who had dropped out of high school, who were judged to be likely to drop out, who were doing satisfactorily in school, and who were doing outstanding work in school. In short, communities can make a significant contribution to the resilience of children.

The communities of Maya, Tobias, Maxine, Richard, and John supported organizations and activities that gave each child an opportunity to develop and demonstrate abilities and skills, be it in school, on a basketball court, during a Boy Scout meeting or a church play. Maya Angelou, Maxine Hong Kingston, Richard Rodriguez, John Wideman, and Tobias Wolff all had opportunities to develop and then demonstrate, publicly, their abilities and talents. Virtually any recent study of youth recognizes the critical importance of self-esteem. To succeed, a child must have a good self image based on the child's belief that she or he is good at something, can do some thing well. Unfortunately, many of the studies that argue for the importance of self-esteem fail to acknowledge that a child develops self-esteem through real achievement and by demonstrating real abilities—not by receiving awards for simply showing up at meetings or trying hard.

There are, of course, a myriad different ways children can demonstrate their talents. For Tobias Wolff, Boy Scouting provided many opportunities and commemorated achievement with merit badges and ranks. For Maya Angelou, opportunities came through church, school and working in a store where adults noticed and praised her competence. John Wideman demonstrated some of his many talents on a basketball court, on a debating team, and in the classroom. And Richard Rodriguez demonstrated his skills by writing in his school and his community newspaper. Indeed, all these children had opportunities to demonstrate publicly their abilities in activities that were supervised by caring adults. None of these children inhabited the adultless world of many contemporary children—a world of solitary television viewing and mindless jobs in stores and restaurants frequented and managed by other young people.

Save for Tobias Wolff, their communities also provided schools that offered each child the opportunity to get a good education and experience success. Maxine Hong Kingston, Maya Angelou, Richard Rodriguez, and John Wideman each attended a better than average school, received extraordinary personal attention from teachers, and achieved uncommon success. John was valedictorian, Maya was salutatorian, and Richard and Maxine graduated at the top of their classes and were admitted to Berkeley and Stanford Universities. Obviously, each of these children inherited extraordinary intellectual powers; one need read only a few pages of any of these autobiographies to recognize this. But often extraordinary skills go to waste because no one notices and nurtures the talents of children.

As noted earlier, the original working title for this study was "The Autobiographies of Desperate Children." The more I worked with the autobiographies, however, the more I realized that this was a poor title. I recognized that the most important commonality of these five works was not the desperation of the children but rather their resilience—the fact that each of them survived difficult childhoods and went on to fruitful and full lives. Moreover, my first title seemed to imply to many people that these children were especially challenged, faced more hardships than all other children. This is not true; many children face far worse challenges than what Maya Angelou or Tobias Wolff faced. Indeed, while I was writing the first draft of this chapter in 1993, *The New York Times* started to run a ten-part series entitled "Children of the Shadows." It is a chilling series, chronicling the extraordinary lives of children who must deal with the most severe problems of our age. One article, for example, profiles the life of Ladeeta Smith, a seventeen year old girl whose mother died of AIDS, whose father died from alcoholism, and who grew up in a project in one of America's worst ghettos, surrounded by violence and drugs. (Lee 1)

Ladeeta Smith lives a far more desperate life than the children whose autobiographies we have read. Maya Angelou, Maxine Kingston, Richard Rodriguez, John Wideman, and Tobias Wolff had family and community support and did not live in poverty. Indeed, each of them lived in families that could afford a well kept apartment or home. Maya's family, through its store, was one of the wealthier

Black families in Stamps. Richard and John's families lived, at least for a while, in homes in the solidly middle class neighborhoods of Pittsburgh and Sacramento. Maxine and Toby's parents live in small homes in solidly working class neighborhoods. Thus each child is exposed to and familiar with middle class lifestyles and, more specifically, white middle class lifestyles. No child experiences the kind of total racial and economic isolation that William Julius Wilson, in *The Truly Disadvantaged* and *When Work Disappears*, argues perpetuates long-term poverty. Thus, a part of the resilience of the authors may certainly also be attributed to financial fortunes of the families of these five children. It is not too glib to state the obvious: very few of the children who have lived the hardest lives and had the least support have been able to write books that testify to their resilience. Indeed, many are dead or in jail or living lives of horrible poverty.

Yet in arguing that Maya Angelou, Maxine Kingston, Richard Rodriguez, John Wideman, and Tobias Wolff were not the most desperate children in America, we should not throw out the baby with the bath water. These five authors did have the advantages of adults who steadfastly cared for them and could provide a roof over their heads and dinner every night and a community that provided them opportunities to demonstrate their talents and taught them something about how the mainstream middle class white population lives. But the hardships these children faced and overcame—rape and physical abuse, absent parents, dysfunctional families, racial, gender, and linguistic discrimination—exceed what most children in America face. In this light, these autobiographies provide a bulwark of hope and a blueprint for the country—for these autobiographies demonstrate that children can overcome many hardships if a little support is forthcoming and if adults are willing to listen and then to act. (I must finish this paragraph by noting that the *Times* profile of Ladeeta Smith is an uplifting story because, after Ladeeta's mother and father died, Ladeeta's grandmother adopted her, took her out of the projects, brought her to live in the struggling but stable and diverse neighborhood of Crown Heights, enrolled her in a strong high school where an assistant principal and an English teacher encouraged her and helped her. In the fall of 1993, Ladeeta Smith enrolled in one of three colleges that admitted her. Here again, then, is another story where a caring female adult, a few stable and caring neighbors, and a strong school with a few committed staff members enable a child to succeed.)

Ultimately, then, these autobiographies and the stories of resilient children should serve as compelling testimony to the great strength of children. From these stories, we can see that many young people can overcome hardships and difficulties. To say that again, in small part for increased clarity and in large part for additional emphasis, these stories of resilience prove that children can overcome a staggering array of obstacles and hardships *as long as families, communities, and institutions provide some of the support that children must have.*

Recently, Norman Garmezy has observed that research has not yet determined what are the most effective ways to build resilience in children. We don't yet know what is most effective and cost efficient. We don't know what activities and institutions are most effective: should we support midnight basketball or camping trips, better schools or stronger churches, peer mentoring or drug abuse counseling. In part, the answers are, of course, contextual. What is helpful for one child would not be as effective to another. Midnight basketball may be effective in my urban community (though no one has ever documented that this is effective), but I doubt it would be effective in my parents' small town in rural, northern New Hampshire (though they recently invested in a lighted skating rink.) The National Urban League points out that the expense of the 100,000 police officers recently hired through federal legislation could have employed 500,000 part time youth workers responsible for developing educational and recreational activities. If each of these 500,000 youth workers reached only ten young people, our nation would have engaged more than five million children in some of the activities that we know build resilience. What is the best investment?

Obviously, there are significant national policy questions involved in the observations above. It seems to me, however, that at the very least, we must debate the issues and recognize that children can be resilient and adults can contribute to this resilience. Or adults can turn their back. I thought again about the importance of adults listening and then getting involved while paging through a recent issue of *Publications of the Modern Language Association of America (PMLA)*. The issue's topic is "Figuring Gender" and the focus is on the trend to "denaturalize the concept of sexual differences and to investigate the cultural construction of men and women." As I interpret it, the issue's goal is to challenge the absolutist paradigm of what is masculine and what is feminine.

I do not question the importance of these issues. They are included in my discussion of the challenges faced by Maxine Hong Kingston (what is feminine? Should she be a house slave or a woman warrior?) and by Tobias Wolff (Is he masculine enough? Can he have Arthur as a friend or must he punch him out publicly?) Yet the writers in *PMLA* never get much beyond word play and obscure works; one argues about the "epistemological importance of triviality and frivolity" in Frank O'Hara's poetry while another draws analogies between early British poetry and the use of make-up. Each author offers readings that are witty and learned and demonstrate the ambiguity of language as well as the power of deconstruction. But to me, each ultimately proves that literary scholarship, at least as it is defined by the Publication of the Modern Languages Association, is for a learned elite who read and write a private language and thereby stay protected, tenured, and well fed within the ivory tower of academia. And it is this very tower that is so unobtainable to so many youth because so few adults have even thought about what they can do to help children.

There are many voices out there—and we must all make choices all the time about who we listen to, what we read, and what we try to achieve. We can spend a lifetime pointing out the ambiguity of language and the importance of frivolity and make-up. We can also spend a lifetime listening to the voices of children and trying to do something that will help all children be successful. Maya Angelou, Maxine Hong Kingston, Richard Rodriguez, John Wideman, Tobias Wolff, Ladeeta Smith, and many, many others give us plenty of hope and plenty to do if we choose to listen.

Selected Bibliography

Abbott, Jack Henry. *In The Belly of the Beast*. New York: Random House, 1984.

Adams, Henry. *The Education of Henry Adams*. Boston: Houghton Mifflin Company, 1918.

Adams, Virginia. "The Sibling Bond: A Lifelong Love/Hate Dialectic." *Psychology Today* June 1981: 30-47.

"After 55 Years." *Newsweek*. 27 December 1962: 46.

Alger, Horatio. *Ragged Dick and Mark, the Match Boy*. New York: Collier Books, 1962.

———. *Wait and Hope: A Plucky Boy's Luck*. New York: New York Book Company, 1910.

Andrews, William. "African-American Autobiography Criticism: Retrospect and Prospect." *American Autobiography*. Ed. John Paul Eakin. Madison: University of Wisconsin Press, 1991. 195-214.

Angelou, Maya. *All God's Children Need Traveling Shoes*. New York: Random House, 1986.

———. *And Still I Rise*. New York: Random House, 1978.

———. *Gather Together in My Name*. New York: Random House, 1974.

———. *The Heart of a Woman*. New York: Random House, 1981.

———. *I Know Why the Caged Bird Sings*. New York, Random House, 1970.

———. *I Shall Not Be Moved*. New York: E.P. Dutton, 1987.

———. *Just Give Me a Cool Drink of Water 'Fore I Diiie*. New York: Random House, 1971.

———. *Now Sheba Sings the Song*. New York: E.P. Dutton, 1987.

———. *Oh Pray My Wings are Gonna Fit Me Well*. New York: Random House, 1975.

———. *Shaker, Why Don't You Sing?*. New York: Random House, 1983.

———. *Singin' and Swingin' and Gettin' Merry Like Christmas*. New York: Random House, 1976.

———. "Shades and Slashes of Light." *Black Women Writers (1950-1980): A Critical Evaluation*. Ed. Mari Evans. Garden City: Anchor-Doubleday, 1984. 3-5.

Anson, Robert Sam. *Best Intentions: The Education and Killing of Edmund Perry*. New York: Random House, 1988.

Anthony, E. James, ed. *The Invulnerable Child*. New York: Guilford Press, 1987.

Arensberg, Liliane. "Death as Metaphor of Self in *I Know Why the Caged Bird Sings*." *College Language Association Journal* 20.2 (1976): 273-291.

Baker, Houston and Redmond, Patricia. *Afro-American Literary Studies in the 1990's*. Chicago: University of Chicago Press, 1991.

Baker, Russell. *Growing Up*. New York: New American Library, 1982.

Baldwin, James. *Go Tell It on the Mountain*. New York: Doubleday and Company, 1952.

Banks, James. "Education, Citizenship, and Cultural Options." *Education and Society* Spring 1988. 19-22.

Barry, Lynda. "Guardian Neighbor." *Newsweek* Summer (Special Issue), 1991. 70-74.

Baym, Nina. "Melodramas of Beset Manhood: How Theories of American Fiction Exclude Women." *The New Feminist Criticism*. Ed. Elaine Showalter. New York: Pantheon Books, 1985. 63-80.

Bell, Robert. "Autobiography and Literary Criticism." *Modern Language Quarterly* 46.2: 191-201.

Bennion, John. "The Shape of Memory in John Edgar Wideman's *Sent For You Yesterday. Black American Literature Forum* 20.1-2: 143-150.

Benstock, Shari, ed. *The Private Self: Theory and Practice of Women's Autobiographical Writings*. Chapel Hill: University of North Carolina Press, 1988.

Berben, Jacqueline. "Beyond Discourse: The Unspoken Versus Words in the Fiction of John Edgar Wideman." *Callaloo* 8.3: 525-534.

Blackburn, Regina. "In Search of the Black Female Self: African American Women's Autobiographies and Ethnicity." *Women's Autobiography*. Ed. Estelle Jelinek. Bloomington: Indiana University Press, 1980.

Blasing, Mutlu. *The Art of Life: Studies in American Autobiographical Literature*. Austin: University of Texas Press, 1977.

Blinde, Patricia. "Icicle in the Desert: Form and Perspective in the Works of Two Chinese American Writers." *MELUS* 6.2 (1979): 51-72.

Bronfenbrenner, Urie. "What Do Families Do?" *Family Affairs* 4.1-2 (1991): 1-6.

Brown, Chip. "Blood Circle." *Esquire* August 1989: 122-132.

Brown, Claude. *Manchild in the Promised Land.* New York: New American Library, 1965.

Bus, Heiner. "Sophisticated Spontaneity: The Art of Life in Gary Soto's *Living Up the Street.*" *The Americas Review* 16.4: 18-29.

Butterfield, Stephen. *Black Autobiography in America.* Amherst: University of Massachusetts Press, 1974.

Campbell, Colin. "The Tyranny of the Yale Critics." *New York Times* 9 February 1986 sec. 6: 20+.

Carter, Forest. *The Education of Little Tree.* Albuquerque: University of New Mexico Press, 1976.

Cary, Lorene. *Black Ice.* New York: Random House, 1991.

Chall, Jeanne. "Rich and Sharp Memories of Reading." *Change* October 1982: 36+.

Cheung, King-kok. "'Don't Tell': Imposed Silences in *The Color Purple* and *The Woman Warrior.*" *PMLA* 103.2 (1988): 162-174.

Ching, Frank. *Ancestors: 900 Years in the Life of a Chinese Family.* New York: Fawcett Columbine, 1988.

Chittenden, Jean. "Toward A Theory of Hispanic Autobiography." *A/B* 10.2 (1988): 1-13.

Chua, Cheng Lok. "Two Chinese Versions of the American Dream: The Gold Mountain in Lin Yutang and Maxine Hong Kingston." *MELUS* 8.2 (1981): 61-70.

Claridge, Laura and Elizabeth Langland, ed. *Out of Bounds: Male Writers and Gender(ed) Criticism.* Amherst: University of Massachusetts Press, 1990.

Clark, Reginald. *Critical Factors in Why Disadvantaged Students Succeed or Fail in School.* New York: Academy for Educational Development, 1988.

———. *Family Life and School Achievement.* Chicago: University of Chicago Press, 1982.

Coe, Richard. *When the Grass Was Taller: Autobiography and the Experience of Childhood.* New Haven: Yale University Press, 1984.

Cohen, Lawrence H., Burt, Charles E., and Bjorck, Jeffrey P. "Life Stress and Adjustment: Effects of Life Events Experienced by Young Adolescents and Their Parents." *Developmental Psychology* 23.4 583-592.

Coleman, James. *Blackness and Modernism: The Literary Career of John Edgar Wideman.* Jackson: University Press of Mississippi, 1989.

Coles, Robert. *Children of Crisis: Volume 1: A Study of Courage and Fear.* Boston: Little, Brown, and Company, 1964.

Comer, James. *Maggie's American Dream.* New York: Penguin, 1988.

Connell, James Patrick et al. "Educational Risk and Resilience in African-American Youth: Context, Self, Action, and Outcomes in School." *Child Development* 65.2 (1994): 493-506.

Conway, Jill Ker. *The Road from Coorain.* New York: Random House, 1989.

Cordell, Shirley. "The Black Woman: A Focus on 'Strength of Character' in *I Know Why the Caged Bird Sings.*" *Virginia English Bulletin* 36.2 (1986): 36-39.

Couser, G. Thomas. *Altered Egos: Authority in American Autobiography.* New York: Oxford University Press, 1989.

Cudjoe, Selwyn. "Maya Angelou and the Autobiographical Statement." *Black Women Writers (1950-1980): A Critical Evaluation.* Ed. Mari Evans. Garden City: Anchor-Doubleday, 1984. 6-23.

Culler, Jonathan. *On Deconstruction.* Ithaca: Cornell University Press, 1982.

Cummins, James. "Empowering Minority Students: A Framework for Intervention." *Harvard Education Review* 56.1 (1986): 18-31.

Dash, Leon. *When Children Want Children.* New York: Penguin Books, 1989.

Davis, Charles and Henry Louis Gates. *The Slave's Narrative.* New York: Oxford University Press, 1985.

De Jesus, Carolina Maria. *Child of the Dark: The Diary of Carolina Maria de Jesus.* New York: New American Library, 1962.

de Man, Paul. "Autobiography as De-Facement." *MLN* 94 (1979): 919-930.

Delpit, Lisa. *Other People's Children: Cultural Conflict in the Classroom.* New York: The New Press, 1995.

Dewey, John. *Experience and Education.* New York: Macmillan, 1938.

Dillard, Annie. *An American Childhood.* New York: Harper & Row, 1987.

Dillon, George. "Whorfian Stylistics." *Journal of Literary Semantics.* 1982: 72-77.

Dohrenwend, Barbara Snell et al. "Symptoms, Hassles, Social Supports, and Life Events: Problem of Confounded Measures." *Journal of Abnormal Psychology.* 93.2: 222- 230.

Donohue, John. "Between Two Worlds." *America* 22 May 1982: 403+.

DuBois, William Edward Burghardt. *The Souls of Black Folk.* New York: New American Library, 1969.

Dugan, Timothy F. and Coles, Robert, ed. *The Child in our times: studies in the development of resiliency.* New York: Brunner/Mazel, 1989.

Dunn, Judy. *Sisters and Brothers*. Cambridge: Harvard University Press, 1985.

Dworkin, Andrea. *Woman Hating*. New York: Dutton, 1979.

Eagleton, Terry. *Literary Theory: An Introduction*. Minneapolis: University of Minnesota, 1983.

———. *Marxism and Literary Criticism*. Berkeley: University of California Press, 1976.

Eakin, John Paul. *American Autobiography: Retrospect and Prospect*. Madison: University of Wisconsin Press, 1989.

———. *Fictions in Autobiography*. Princeton: Princeton University Press, 1985.

Edelman, Marian Wright. *The Measure of Our Success*. Boston: Beacon Press, 1992.

Egan, Susanna. *Patterns of Experience in Autobiography*. Chapel Hill: University of North Carolina Press, 1984.

Elliot, Jeffrey. *Conversations with Maya Angelou*. Jackson: University Press of Mississippi, 1989.

Ellison, Ralph. *Invisible Man*. New York: Random House, 1947.

Evans, Mari. ed. *Black Women Writers (1950-1980): A Critical Evaluation*. Garden City: Anchor-Doubleday, 1984.

Evans, Thomas. *Mentors*. Princeton: Peterson's Guides, 1992.

Fiske, Edward. *Smart Schools, Smark Kids*. New York: Simon and Schuster, 1991.

Fonagy, Peter et al. "The Theory and Practice of Resilience." *Journal of Child Psychology and Psychiatry*. 35.2: 231-57.

Foucault, Michel. *Discipline and Punish*. New York: Random House, 1979.

Freedman, Samuel. *Small Victories*. New York: Harper & Row, 1990.

Friedman, Susan Stanford. "Women's Autobiographical Selves: Theory and Practice" *The Private Self: Theory and Practice of Women's Autobiographical Writings*. Ed. Shari Benstock. Chapel Hill: University of North Carolina, 1988. 34-62.

Froula, Christine. "The Daughter's Seduction: Sexual Violence and Literary History." *Signs* 11.4 (1986): 621-644.

Frye, Joanne. "*The Woman Warrior*: Claiming Narrative Power, Recreating Female Selfhood." *Faith of a (Woman) Writer*. Ed. Alice Kessler-Harris. Westport: Greenwood, 1988. 293-301.

Galarza, Ernesto. *Barrio Boy*. Notre Dame: University of Notre Dame Press, 1981.

Gardner, John. *On Moral Fiction*. New York: Basic Books, 1978.

Garmezy, Norman. "Children in Poverty: resilience despite risk." *Psychiatry* 56 (Feb. 93): 127-136.

———. "Resiliency and Vulnerability to Adverse Developmental Outcomes Associated with Poverty." *American Behavioral Scientist* 34.4: 416-430.

——— and Ann S. Masten and Auke Tellegen. "The Study of Stress and Competence in Children: A Building Block for Developmental Psychopathology." *Child Development* 55 (1984).1: 97-111.

——— and Michael Rutter, eds. *Stress, coping, and development in children.* New York: McGraw-Hill, 1983.

Gates, Henry Louis. *The Signifying Monkey*. Oxford: Oxford University Press, 1988.

Gilead, Sarah. "Emigrant Selves: Narrative Strategies in Three Women's Autobiographies." *Criticism* 30.1 (1988): 43-62.

Gilman, David. "The Miracle of Resiliency." *Newsweek* v. 117 (Special Issue, Summer, 1991): 44-47.

Gorbea-Leon, Dana. "Richard Rodriguez's Stereotypes." *Harper's* January 1991: 2-3.

Gregory, Lynn W. "The 'Turnaround' Process: Factors Influencing the School Success of Urban Youth." *Journal of Adolescent Research* 10.1: 136-154.

Gubar, Susan. "'The Blank Page' and the Issues of Female Creativity." *The New Feminist Criticism*. Ed. Elaine Showalter. New York: Pantheon Books, 1985. 292-314.

Haley, Alex. *The Autobiography of Malcolm X*. New York: Ballantine Books, 1964.

Holte, James Craig. *The Ethnic I: A Sourcebook for Ethnic-American Autobiography*. New York: Greenwood Press, 1988.

———. "Private lives and public faces: Ethnic American Autobiography." *Ethnic Groups* 4.1 (1982): 61-83.

———. "The Representative Voice: Autobiography and the Ethnic Experience." *MELUS* 9.2 (1981): 25-46.

Hunt, Linda. "'I Could Not Figure Out What Was My Village': Gender Vs. Ethnicity in Maxine Hong Kingston's *The Woman Warrior*." *MELUS* 12.3 (1985): 5-12.

Hurston, Zora Neale. *Dust Tracks on a Road*. Urbana: University of Illinois Press, 1984.

Irujo, Suzanne. "Do You Know Why They All Talk At Once." *Equity and Choice* May, 1989.

Jelinek, Estelle. *Women's Autobiography*. Bloomington: Indiana University Press, 1980.

Johnson, James Weldon. *The Autobiography of an Ex-Coloured Man*. New York: Hill and Wang, 1960.

Kent, George. "Maya Angelou's *I Know Why the Caged Bird Sings* and Black Autobiographical Tradition." *Kansas Quarterly* 7.3 (1975): 72-78.

Kidder, Tracy. *Among Schoolchildren*. Boston: Houghton, Mifflin, 1986.

Kiell, Norman. *Blood Brothers: Siblings as Writers*. New York: International University Press, 1987.

Kincaid, Jamaica. *A Small Place*. New York: Farrar, Straus, and Giroux, 1988.

Kingston, Maxine Hong. *China Men*. New York: Random House, 1977.

———. "Cultural Mis-Readings by American Reviewers." *Asian and Western Writers in Dialogue: New Cultural Identities*. Ed. Guy Amirthanayagam. London: Macmillan, 1982. 55-65.

———. *Hawai'i One Summer*. New York: Random House, 1987.

———. *Tripmaster Monkey*. New York: Random House, 1987.

———. *The Woman Warrior*. New York: Random House, 1976.

Kinnamon, Kenneth. "Call and Response: Intertextuality in Two Autobiographical Works by Wright and Maya Angelou." *Belief vs. Theory in Black American Literary Criticism*. Ed. Weixlmann. Greenwood: Penkeville, 1986. 121-134.

Knowles, John. *A Separate Peace*. New York: Macmillan Company, 1959.

Kotlowitz, Alex. *There Are No Children Here*. New York: Doubleday, 1991.

Kozol, Jonathan. *death at an early age*. Boston: Houghton- Mifflin, 1967.

———. *Savage Inequalities*. New York: Crown Publishers, 1991.

Lanham, Richard. *Analyzing Prose*. New York: Scribners, 1983.

Lau, Joseph. "Kingston as Exorcist." *Modern Chinese Writers: Critical Appraisals*. Ed. Michael Duke. Armonk: Sharpe, 1989. 44-52.

Lazarus, Richard S et al. "Stress and Adaptational Outcomes: The Problem of Confounded Measures." *American Psychologist* 40.7: 770-780.

Lee, Felicia. "With No Parents, Ladeeta, 18, Presses On." *New York Times* 6 April 1993: 1+

Lejeune, Philippe. *On Autobiography*. Minneapolis: University of Minnesota Press, 1989.

Li, David Leiwei. "The Naming of a Chinese American "I": Cross-Cultural Sign/ifications in *The Woman Warrior*. *Criticism* 30.4 (1988): 497-515.

Lukas, J. Anthony. *Common Ground*. New York: Random House, 1986.

Luthar, Suniya and Zigler, Edward. "Vulnerability and Resilience: A Review of Research on Resilience in Childhood." *American Journal of Orthopsychiatry* 61.1: 6-22.

Mack, John E and Holly Hickler. *Vivienne: The Life and Suicide of an Adolescent Girl*. New York: New American Library, 1981.

Maclean, Norman. *A River Runs Through It and Other Stories*. Chicago: University of Chicago Press, 1976.

Mailer, Norman. Introduction. *In The Belly of the Beast*. Jack Henry Abbott. New York: Vintage Books, 1982.

Markus, Hazel. "Sibling Personalities: The Luck of the Draw." *Psychology Today* June 1981: 35+.

Marquez, Antonio. "Richard Rodriguez's *Hunger of Memory* and the Poetics of Experience." *Arizona Quarterly* 40.2: 130- 142.

Marshall, Paule. *Brown Girl, Brownstones*. New York: The Feminist Press, 1981.

Masten, Ann S and Karin M. Best and Norman Garmezy. "Resilience and development: Contributions from the study of children who overcome adversity." *Development and Psychopathology* 1990.2: 425-445.

McIntosh, Cary. "Quantities of Qualities: Nominal Style and the Novel." *Studies in Eighteenth-Century Culture* 4.1 (1975): 139-152.

McPherson, Dolly. *Order Out of Chaos: The Autobiographical Works of Maya Angelou*. New York: Lang, 1989.

Meier, Kenneth. *Race, Class, and Education: The Politics of Second-Generation Discrimination*. Madison: University of Wisconsin Press, 1989.

Miller, Margaret. "Threads of Identity in Maxine Hong Kingston's *Woman Warrior*." *biography* 6.1: 13-33.

Monmaney, Terence. "Kids Who Bounce Back." *Newsweek* 12 September 1988: 67.

Moody, Anne. *Coming of Age in Mississippi*. New York: Dell Publishing Company, 1968.

Morrison, Toni. *Sula*. New York: New American Library, 1973.

———. *The Bluest Eye*. New York: Washington Square Press, 1970.

Mulholland, Debra Japzon and Norman Watt. "Academic Performance in Children of Divorce: Psychological Resilience and Vulnerability." *Psychiatry* 54.8 (August 1991): 268-280.

Nadel, Ira Bruce. *Biography: Fiction, Fact and Form*. New York: St. Martin's Press, 1984.

Neubauer, Carol. "Displacement and Autobiographical Style in Maya Angelou's *The Heart of a Woman. Black American Literature Forum* 17.3 (1983): 123-129.

Oates, Joyce Carol. *Them*. New York: Fawcett Crest, 1969.

Olivas, Michael. "Painful to Write, Painful to Read." *Change* October 1982: 37+.

Olney, James, ed. *Essays Theoretical and Critical.* Princeton: Princeton University Press, 1980.

O'Neale, Sondra. "Reconstruction of the Composite Self: New Images of Black Women in Maya Angelou's Continuing Autobiography." *Black Women Writers (1950-1980): A Critical Evaluation.* Ed. Mari Evans. Garden City: Anchor-Doubleday, 1984. 25-36.

Ordonez, Elizabeth. "Narrative Texts by Ethnic Women: Rereading The Past, Reshaping The Future." *MELUS* 9.3 (1982): 19-28.

Owens, William. *This Stubborn Soil.* New York: Random House, 1989.

Pines, Maya. "Superkids." *Psychology Today* Jan, 1979: 53- 63.

Poussaint, Alvin. "Building a Positive Self-Image in a Black Child." *Ebony* February 1985: 25+.

Pryse, Marjorie and Hortense Spillers, eds. *Conjuring: Black Women, Fiction, and Literary Tradition.* Bloomington: Indiana University Press. 1985.

Rabine, Leslie. "No Lost Paradise: Social Gender and Symbolic Gender in the Writings of Maxine Hong Kingston." *Signs* 12.3 (1987): 471-492.

Rampersad, Arnold. "Biography, Autobiography, and Afro- American Culture." *The Yale Review* 73.1 (1978): 1-16.

Rause, Vince. "Brothers and Keepers." *Saturday Review* November/December 1984: 51-56.

Rayson, Ann. "Beneath the Mask: Autobiographies of Japanese- American Women." *MELUS* 14.1 (1987): 43-57.

Redmond, Eugene. "Boldness of Language and Breadth: An Interview with Maya Angelou." *Black American Literature Forum* 22.2 (1988): 156-157.

Reed, Ishmael. "Of One Blood, Two Men." *New York Times* 4 November 1984, sec 7: 1+.

Rivera, Tomas. "Richard Rodriguez's *Hunger of Memory* as Humanistic Antithesis." *MELUS* 11.4: 5-13.

Rodriguez, Richard. *Days of Obligation: An Argument with my Mexican Father*. New York: Penguin, 1992.

———. "Fear of Losing A Culture." *Time* 11 July 1988: 84.

———. *Hunger of Memory: The Education of Richard Rodriguez*. New York: Bantam Books, 1982.

———. "A Minority Scholar Speaks Out." *American Education* November 1982: 32-33.

———. "True West." *Harpers* 293:1756 (Sept 1996): 37-46.

Rose, Mike. *Lives on the Boundaries*. New York: Penguin Books, 1990.

Rose, Shirley. "Metaphors and Myths of Cross-Cultural Literacy: Autobiographical Narratives by Maxine Hong Kingston, Richard Rodriguez, and Malcolm X." *MELUS* 14.1 (1987): 3-15.

Rowlinson, Richard and Robert Fellner. "Major Life Events, Hassles, and Adaptation in Adolescence: Confounding in the Conceptualization and Measurement of Life Stress and Adjustment Revisited." Journal of Personality and Social Psychology 55.3: 432-444.

Rubin, Steven. "Ethnic Autobiography: A Comparative Approach." *Journal of Ethnic Studies* 9.1 (1981): 78-79.

Ryan, Michael. *Secret Life*. New York: Pantheon Books, 1995.

Ryan, William. *Blaming the Victim*. New York: Random House, 1971.

Saldivar, Ramon. *Chicano Narrative: The Dialectics of Difference*. Madison: University of Wisconsin Press, 1990.

———. "Ideologies of the Self: Chicano Autobiography." *Diacritics* 5.3 (1985): 27-34.

Salinger, J.D. *The Catcher in the Rye*. New York: Little, Brown, and Company, 1951.

Samuels, Wilfred. "Going Home: A Conversation with John Edgar Wideman." *Callaloo* 6.1: 40-59.

"Scholarships: Two for the Fight." *Time* 28 December 1962: 55.

Scholes, Robert. *Protocols of Reading*. New Haven: Yale University Press, 1989.

———. *Textual Power*. New Haven: Yale University Press, 1985.

Schorr, Lisbeth. *Within Our Reach: Breaking the Cycle of Disadvantage*. New York: Doubleday, 1988.

Schueller, Malini. "Questioning Race and Gender Definitions: Dialogic Subversions in *The Woman Warrior*." *Criticism* 31.4 (1989): 421-437.

Shakur, Sanyika. *Monster: The Autobiography of an LA Gang Member*. New York: Penguin, 1993.

Shalit, Gene. "The Astonishing John Wideman." *Look* 21 May 1963: 30-36.

Shaughnessy, Mina. *Errors and Expectations*. New York: Oxford University Press, 1977.

Showalter, Elaine, ed. *The New Feminist Criticism*. New York: Pantheon Books, 1985.

Sizer, Theodore. *Horace's Compromise*. Boston: Houghton Mifflin, 1984.

———. *Horace's School*. Boston: Houghton Mifflin, 1992.

Smith, Sidonie. *A Poetics of Women's Autobiography*. Bloomington: Indiana University Press, 1987.

———. "The Song of a Caged Bird: Maya Angelou's Quest after Self-Acceptance." *Southern Humanities Review*. 7.2 (1973): 365-375.

Smith, Valerie. *Self Discovery and Authority in Afro-American Narrative*. Cambridge: Harvard University Press, 1987.

Soto, Gary, ed. *California Childhood*. Berkeley: Creative Arts Book Company, 1988.

———. *Living Up the Street*. San Francisco: Strawberry Hill Press, 1985.

Stepto, Robert. *From Behind the Veil: A Study of Afro- American Narrative*. Urbana: University of Illinois Press, 1979.

Stoltenberg, John. *Refusing to be a man*. New York: Penguin, 1989.

Stone, Alfred. "After *Black Boy* and *Dusk of Dawn*: Patterns in Recent Black Autobiography." *Phylon* 39.1 (1978): 1978.

———, ed. *The American Autobiography: A Collection of Critical Essays*. Englewood Cliffs: Prentice Hall, 1981.

———. *Autobiographical Occasions and Original Acts: Versions of American Identity from Henry Adams to Nate Shaw*. Philadelphia: University of Pennsylvania Press, 1982.

———. "Collaboration in Contemporary Autobiography." *Revue Francaise d'Etudes Americaines* 7.14 (1982): 151-165.

Stone, Elizabeth. *Black Sheep and Kissing Cousins: How Our Family Stories Shape Us*. New York: Penguin, 1988.

Tate, Claudia. "Maya Angelou." *Black Women Writers at Work*. Ed. Claudia Tate. New York: Continuum, 1983. 1-11.

Taylor, Gordon. "Voices from the Veil: Black American Autobiography." *Georgia Review* 35.4 (1981): 341-361.

Taylor, Talbott. *Linguistic Theory and Structural Stylistics*. York: Pergaman Press, 1981.

Thomas, Piri. *Down These Mean Streets*. New York: Random House, 1984.

Thompson, Phyllis Hoge. "This is the Story I Heard: A Conversation with Maxine Hong Kingston and Earll Kingston." *biography* 6.1 (1983): 1-12.

Toth, Susan Allen. *Blooming: A Small-Town Girlhood*. New York: Ballantine Books, 1978.

Twain, Mark. *The Adventures of Huckleberry Finn*. New York: Bantam Books, 1985.

Vaillant, George E. *The Wisdom of the Ego*. Cambridge, MA: Harvard University Press, 1993.

Villanueva-Collado, Alfredo. "Growing Up Hispanic: Discourse and Ideology in *Hunger of Memory* and *Family Installments*." *The Americas Review* 16.3-4: 75-90.

Walker, Alice. *The Color Purple*. New York: Washington Square Press, 1982.

Wang, Alfred. "Maxine Hong Kingston's Reclaiming of America: The Birthright of the Chinese American Male." *South Dakota Review* 26.1 (1988): 18-29.

Wang, Veronica. "Reality and Fantasy: The Chinese-American Woman's Quest for Identity." *MELUS* 12.3 (1985): 23-31.

Wehlage, Gary et. al. *Reducing the Risk: Schools as Communities of Support*. New York: Falmer Press, 1989.

Weintraub, Karl Joachim. *The Value of the Individual: Self and Circumstance in Autobiography*. Chicago: University of Chicago Press, 1978.

Werner, Emmy and Ruth Smith. *Overcoming the Odds: High Risk Children from Birth to Adulthood*. Ithaca: Cornell University Press, 1992.

——— and Ruth Smith. *Vulnerable but Invincible: A Study of Resilient Children*. New York: McGraw-Hill, 1982.

Wheelock, Anne. *Crossing the Tracks*. New York: The New Press, 1992.

White, Edmund. *A Boy's Own Story*. New York: New American Library, 1982.

Wideman, John Edgar. *A Glance Away*. New York: Holt, Rinehart and Winston, 1967.

———. "The Black Writer and the Magic of the Word." *New York Times* 24 January 1988 sec. 7: 1+.

———. *Brothers and Keepers*. New York: Random House, 1984.

———. *Damballah*. New York: Avon, 1981.

———. *Fatheralong*. New York: Random House: 1994.

———. *Fever*. New York: Henry Holt and Company, 1990.

———. *Hiding Place*. New York: Random House, 1981.

———. *The Homewood Trilogy: Damballah, Hiding Place, and Sent for You Yesterday*. New York: Avon, 1985.

———. *Hurry Home*. New York: Henry Holt and Company, 1970.

———. *The Lynchers*. New York: Henry Holt and Company, 1973.

———. *Philadelphia Fire*. New York: Henry Holt and Company, 1990.

———. Preface. *Breaking Ice*. ed. Terry McMillan. New York: Penguin, 1990.

———. "Publish and Still Perish: The Dilemma of Black Educators on White Campuses." *Black Enterprise* September 1981: 45-49.

———. *Reuben*. New York: Penguin Books, 1987.

———. *Sent For You Yesterday*. New York: Avon, 1983.

Will, George F. "Hunger of Memory." *The Washington Post* 14 February 1982 sec. 6: 8+.

Williams, Raymond. *Marxism and Literature*. Oxford: Oxford University Press, 1977.

Wilson, William Julius. *The Truly Disadvantaged: The Inner City, The Underclass, and Public Policy*. Chicago: University of Chicago Press, 1987.

Wolff, Geoffrey. *The Duke of Deception*. New York: Penguin, 1986.

Wolff, Tobias. *Back in the World*. New York: Houghton Mifflin, 1985.

———. *The Barracks Thief and Selected Stories*. New York: Echo Press, 1981.

———. *In the Garden of the North American Martyrs*. New York: Echo Press, 1976.

———. *This Boy's Life*. New York: Harper & Row, 1989.

Wong, Jade Snow. *Fifth Chinese Daughter*. Seattle: University of Washington Press, 1989.

Woods, Richard. "Mexican Autobiography in English." *A/B* 3.4: 62-64.

———. "An Overview of Mexican Autobiography." *A/B* 3.4 (1988): 13-20.

Wright, Richard. *Native Son*. New York: Harper and Row, 1940.

Zweig, Paul. "The Child of Two Cultures." *New York Times* 28 February, 1982, Book Section: 1.

Zweigenhaft, Richard and William G. Domhoff. *Blacks in the White Establishment?* New Haven: Yale University Press, 1991.

Index

For Product Safety Concerns and Information please contact our EU representative GPSR@taylorandfrancis.com
Taylor & Francis Verlag GmbH, Kaufingerstraße 24, 80331 München, Germany

www.ingramcontent.com/pod-product-compliance
Lightning Source LLC
Chambersburg PA
CBHW071402100726
47908CB00004B/1069

* 9 7 8 0 3 6 7 3 3 4 2 0 8 *